Understanding the U.S. Constitution

By Mark Stange

COPYRIGHT © 1994 Mark Twain Media, Inc.

ISBN 1–58037–056–X

Printing No. CD-1831

Mark Twain Media, Inc., Publishers
Distributed by Carson-Dellosa Publishing Company, Inc.

INTRODUCTION

There is nothing more important to the future of America than producing good citizens. In order to be good citizens, we must first gain a basic understanding of the document that created our government: the Constitution of the United States.

This activity book is designed to give students a brief overview of the Constitution. There are short readings followed by questions and activities. The Constitution is located at the end of the book, and those portions that are no longer in effect are shown in italicized print. The sample test included measures the students' knowledge of the Constitution.

American history is an extremely important subject to study if we wish to continue the way of life we enjoy as Americans. Imagine life without a President or Congress, or without the freedom of religion or speech. In order to pass these freedoms on to future generations, we must first learn about and defend them.

TABLE OF CONTENTS

TABLE OF CONTENTS (continued)

THE BIRTH OF THE CONSTITUTION

The Articles of Confederation

During the Revolutionary War, the United Colonies needed a document to govern the lands then struggling to be free from England's rule. The Articles of Confederation became the first national constitution of the United States in March of 1781.

The Articles of Confederation established a government organized around a Congress. Each of the thirteen states would only have one vote regardless of size or population. For a law to pass, nine of the thirteen states had to agree.

The Congress had the power to declare war, make peace, and make treaties. It could also coin and borrow money, create post offices, admit new states, and create an army and navy.

On the other hand, the Congress could not tax, and it could not control or interfere with trade between the individual states.

There was no one person who was in charge of this new government. Because they feared the return of tyranny, the founding fathers were very cautious not to create a new "king"—that was exactly why they had separated from England. So, as a result, there was no executive to carry out the laws passed by Congress. Ultimately, this lack of a leader caused much confusion.

The Articles of Confederation created a loose friendship between the thirteen states. This loose friendship

Revolutionary War Soldiers

was enough to win the War for Independence and keep the states together as one country. But without an executive, the power to tax, and the ability to regulate trade, the Congress could not function effectively. Many Americans felt the Articles of Confederation needed to be revised.

By 1786, more problems were beginning to surface. A convention of five of the thirteen states, called the Annapolis Convention, met at Annapolis, Maryland, in September, 1786. They met to study the trade problem. There was not enough representation to make any big decisions, so the delegates led by Alexander Hamilton (New York) and James Madison (Virginia) called for another convention to begin in May, 1787, in Philadelphia, Pennsylvania. In February of that year, Congress agreed with the delegates and stated the convention would have the "sole and express purpose of revising the Articles of Confederation."

Date _____   Name _____

THE BIRTH OF THE CONSTITUTION
The Articles of Confederation
≈ **Challenges** ≈

1. Define:
   Confederation: _____

   _____

   Constitution: _____

   _____

   Commerce: _____

   _____

2. What was the first form of our national government? _____

   _____

3. When did our first form of government begin to govern the United States? _____

   _____

4. For a law to pass, how many states had to agree? _____

5. What were the powers of Congress under the Articles of Confederation? _____

   _____

6. What could Congress **NOT** do under the Articles? _____

   _____

7. Why was there no executive under the Articles? _____

   _____

8. What meeting occurred in September, 1786? What was its purpose? _____

   _____

   _____

9. What was scheduled to happen in May, 1787? Why? _____

   _____

   _____

The Constitutional Convention

The Constitutional Convention opened in Philadelphia in May, 1787, and finished its work in September. The delegates to the convention were not elected by the people, but instead were selected by their state legislatures.

The delegates to the convention were men of great ability. Many had fought in the Revolutionary War, many were educated, and many were wealthy. They were men of great power and influence in their own states. Eventually, two would become presidents of the United States, one a vice president, and 26 would serve in Congress. All in all, there were 65 official delegates, but only 55 made it to Philadelphia. The average attendance at each day's meeting was about 30.

George Washington, a delegate from Virginia, was chosen to be the president of the convention. At first, the purpose of the convention was to revise the Articles of Confederation, but very quickly the delegates decided to replace the Articles with a new plan for government.

Two important leaders were absent from the convention. John Adams and Thomas Jefferson, who were influential in the writing of the Declaration of Independence, were in Europe serving as ambassadors to other nations. Benjamin Franklin of Pennsylvania was the oldest delegate at 81 years old, and

George Washington was chosen as the president of the Constitutional Convention.

Jonathan Dayton of New Jersey was the youngest at 26. Other delegates present were Alexander Hamilton and James Madison. There was one state that refused to send delegates to the Constitutional Convention; Rhode Island did not send any representatives to Philadelphia.

During those five hot summer months in 1787, the 55 delegates struggled to create a more flexible form of government for the new United States. The most serious task that faced the delegates was how to achieve a balance between liberty and authority. There were many different viewpoints and opinions on how to go about that task. The concept of compromise unified the differences into a supreme document capable of representing the opinions of all Americans.

The Constitution that resulted from this historic convention is now over 200 years old. Few written constitutions have lasted as long as the Constitution of the United States.

THE BIRTH OF THE CONSTITUTION
The Constitutional Convention
≈ Challenges ≈

1. Define:
    Convention: _____

    _____

    Compromise: _____

    _____

    Delegate: _____

    _____

2. Where did the Constitutional Convention meet in May, 1787? _____

    _____

3. During what months of 1787 was our Constitution written? _____

    _____

4. Which state didn't send delegates to the Convention? _____

5. Who served as president of the convention? _____

6. What was the most serious task that the convention faced? _____

    _____

7. Name two famous politicians who were present at the convention. _____

    _____

8. Name two famous politicians who were absent from the convention. _____

    _____

9. Who was the oldest delegate? _____

10. Who was the youngest delegate? _____

Compromise

Without compromise in 1787, our government would have collapsed in infancy. Compromise is a settlement in which both sides give up something in order to reach an agreement. There were many different compromises made during the Constitutional Convention. The most important compromises dealt with how our government would be set up.

A major concern of the delegates was how to set up the lawmaking body of our government, the legislative branch. How should states be represented in the legislative body? Who would have control—the small states or the large states? This issue threatened to destroy the convention. Eventually, the delegates came to an agreement known as the Great Compromise, which combined the best of the Virginia Plan and the New Jersey Plan.

The Virginia Plan was proposed by the states having the larger populations. First, they suggested that the lawmaking body be called Congress. This Congress was to be *bicameral* (having two houses). The first house would be elected by the people, and the second house would be elected by the

The Convention was held in the Philadelphia Statehouse, now known as Independence Hall.

first house. The number of Congressmen was to be determined by the population of the state. The larger states liked this plan because they had a larger population and as a result would be able to control the government. They favored a plan based on population.

An alternative was the New Jersey Plan supported by the smaller states. First, the small states proposed a Congress that was *unicameral* (having one house) with each state having the same number of representatives or votes. The smaller states would then be equal with the larger states. They favored a plan based on equality.

Eventually a compromise was reached. The compromise became known as the Great Compromise, because without this basic issue settled, the Convention would have failed.

The Great Compromise called for a bicameral Congress. The first house was to be called the House of Representatives, with representatives elected by the people for a two-year term. The number of representatives each state could elect would depend on the population of the state. This pleased the large states.

The second house was to be called the Senate, with senators elected by their state legislatures for a six-year term. Each state would have two senators. This pleased the small states. The Great Compromise had succeeded; both sides got what they wanted.

Date _____ Name _____

THE BIRTH OF THE CONSTITUTION

Compromise
≈ **Challenges** ≈

1. Define:
   Bicameral: _____

   Unicameral: _____

2. What question was resolved with the Great Compromise? _____

   _____

3. What plan was supported by the large states? Why? _____

   _____

4. What plan was supported by the small states? Why? _____

   _____

5. Fill in the information:

   A. Virginia Plan:
      1. How many houses? _____

      2. Number of congressmen determined by: _____

   B. New Jersey Plan:
      1. How many houses? _____

      2. Number of congressmen determined by: _____

6. What was the Great Compromise, and how did it establish the legislative body?

   _____

   _____

   _____

7. Circle the correct ending to each statement:
   A. Representatives in the House of Representatives are chosen by:
            POPULATION   EQUALITY

   B. Senators in the Senate are chosen by:
            POPULATION   EQUALITY

Separation of Powers

Another problem facing the Constitutional Convention was how to divide the powers of a government. Who will make the laws? Who will make sure the laws are obeyed? Who will make sure the laws are "good" laws? These questions were answered in the next set of compromises.

American government can be seen as a tree. The Constitution is the trunk, or base, with three branches extending from that trunk. Those three branches are the legislative branch, the executive branch, and the judicial branch. Each branch has different responsibilities and looks out for and checks the other two branches. These concepts, respectively, are called *separation of powers* and *checks and balances.*

The *legislative* branch was defined during the Great Compromise. Together, the House of Representatives and the Senate make the laws to govern our country. The legislative branch also checks the executive and judicial branches.

The second branch is the *executive* branch. Eventually, the delegates decided to create a chief executive. Under the Articles of Confederation, there was no national leader. The founding fathers had feared creating another "king." There was much discussion, even talk of having two

The U.S. Constitution provides for the legislative, executive, and judicial branches of government.

equally powered leaders. The convention agreed to create one President, but only if the President would be checked or watched by the legislative and judicial branches. The job of the President and the executive branch is to carry out the laws passed by the legislative branch.

The third branch established the *judicial* system. The judicial branch was to be headed by the Supreme Court. It is the job of the Supreme Court to interpret or define the laws. The Supreme Court is chosen by the President and approved by the Senate. The judicial branch checks the executive and legislative branches.

Each branch has its own specific responsibilities. Each has a separate power. Part of the responsibility of a branch is to control or check the power of the other branches. That way, no one branch gets to be too powerful; each branch is balanced.

Date _____   Name _____

THE BIRTH OF THE CONSTITUTION

Separation of Powers
≈ **Challenges** ≈

1. Define:

Separation of Powers: _____

Checks and Balances: _____

Legislative: _____

Executive: _____

Judicial: _____

2. Name three ways in which the powers of the United States are divided.

_____

_____

_____

3. Why are the powers separated? _____

_____

4. What is the job of the legislative branch? _____

_____

5. What is the job of the executive branch? _____

_____

6. What is the job of the judicial branch? _____

_____

7. What two branches are checked by the legislative branch? _____

_____

8. What two branches are checked by the executive branch? _____

_____

9. What two branches are checked by the judicial branch? _____

_____

Organization of the Constitution

On September 17, 1787, the Constitutional Convention approved the Constitution of the United States. The document was then sent out to the states to be *ratified*, or approved, through a specific procedure set up in the Constitution. On June 21, 1788, New Jersey became the ninth state to ratify the Constitution, and the necessary three-fourths majority was achieved. The United States began to function under a new form of government.

The Constitution is divided into several parts. It starts with the *Preamble,* or introduction. The main body of the document consists of seven *Articles.* The final section of the Constitution contains the *Amendments*, or changes to the Constitution. There are presently 27 Amendments.

The first three Articles deal with the three separate branches of government. The last four Articles discuss the powers of the states and the procedures for ratifying and amending the Constitution. Each Article is further subdivided into Sections and then into Clauses.

On your copy of the Constitution you will notice that some phrases or sections are printed in *italics.* This indicates that these parts are no longer in effect due to the passage of time or changes made by the Amendments.

On the next page is a chart of the organization of the Constitution.

Throughout the convention Ben Franklin had noticed the back of George Washington's chair. There was a sun carved into it. "I have often and often in the course of this session looked at that behind the President without being able to tell whether it was rising or setting; but now at length I have the happiness to know that it is a rising and not a setting sun," Franklin observed.

9

Organization of the Constitution

PREAMBLE   Introduction

ARTICLE I   Legislative Branch
ARTICLE II   Executive Branch
ARTICLE III   Judicial Branch
ARTICLE IV   Relationships Among States
ARTICLE V   Amending the Constitution
ARTICLE VI   Supreme Law of the Land
ARTICLE VII   Ratifying the Constitution

AMENDMENTS:

I	Freedom of religion, press, speech, assembly, petition
II	Right to bear arms
III	Quartering of soldiers
IV	Searches and seizures
V	Life, liberty, and property
VI	Rights of the accused
VII	Right to trial by jury
VIII	Bail and punishment
IX	Rights of the people
X	Rights of the states
XI	Suits against states
XII	Election of the President
XIII	Abolition of slavery
XIV	Civil rights in the states
XV	Black suffrage
XVI	Income tax
XVII	Direct election of senators
XVIII	Prohibition
XIX	Women's suffrage
XX	"Lame duck" period
XXI	Repeal of Prohibition
XXII	Presidential term of office
XXIII	Voting in the District of Columbia
XXIV	Abolition of poll taxes
XXV	Presidential disability and succession
XXVI	Eighteen-year-old vote
XXVII	Congressional pay raises

Date _____ Name _____

THE BIRTH OF THE CONSTITUTION

Organization of the Constitution
≈ Challenges ≈

1. Define:
   Ratify: _____

   Amend: _____

   Article: _____

2. When was the Constitution approved by the Convention? _____

3. What date was the Constitution approved by the states? _____

4. What do you think the sun represents in Franklin's quotation? _____

   _____

5. What is the purpose of the Preamble? _____

   _____

6. How many Articles are in the Constitution? _____

7. What is Article I about? _____

   _____

. . . Article II? _____

   _____

. . . Article III? _____

   _____

8. How many Amendments have been added to the Constitution? _____

   _____

9. Why have certain phrases or sections been italicized? _____

   _____

   _____

The Preamble
(See the Preamble)

The Preamble lists the major goals to be accomplished by the United States government under the Constitution. The importance of the Preamble and the Constitution are expressed in the first three words, "We the people . . . ." The Constitution was created by the people, not by some king, dictator, or absolute ruler.

The founding fathers had six goals in mind when they set out to create the Constitution. They are:

(1) to form a more perfect union
   (set up a stronger government than they had under the Articles of Confederation)
(2) establish justice
   (improve the court system)
(3) insure domestic tranquility
   (have peace in all states)
(4) provide for the common defense
   (protect the country from enemies)
(5) promote the general welfare
   (have good living conditions)
(6) secure the blessings of liberty to ourselves and our posterity.
   (have freedom for themselves and future Americans)

The Preamble expresses the hopes of the people for a good and honest government for themselves and their children.

PREAMBLE TO THE UNITED STATES CONSTITUTION:

We the people of the United States, in order to form a more perfect Union, Establish Justice, insure domestic Tranquility, provide for the common Defense, promote the general Welfare, and secure the blessings of Liberty to ourselves and our Posterity, do ordain and establish this Constitution for the United States of America.

THE BIRTH OF THE CONSTITUTION

The Preamble
≈ Challenges ≈

1. By whose power was the Constitution written? _____

2. Fill in the blanks:

GOALS OF THE CONSTITUTION:

(Actual words of the Constitution)   (Your own words)

a. _____   _____

b. _____   _____

c. _____   _____

d. _____   _____

e. _____   _____

f. _____   _____

3. Rewrite the Preamble in your own words.

_____

_____

_____

_____

_____

_____

_____

_____

_____

_____

_____

_____

PROJECTS:

1. The Preamble is short, only 52 words. Memorize and recite it to the class. (Extra: do it in only one breath!)

2. Bring a copy of a student organization constitution to class. How is it similar to or different from the U. S. Constitution?

THE LEGISLATIVE BRANCH

Introduction

(See Article I, Section 1)

The legislative branch of the United States government is described in Article I of the Constitution. Its major job is to make our country's laws. The American system of government is based on a representative form of government. Not all Americans can meet in the same place at the same time to make laws, so Americans choose representatives to make the laws for them. Representatives carry out the will of the people, or they are replaced during the next election.

Laws are passed by a *majority* vote. Majority means one over half. For example, among 10 people, six or more of them must agree in order to pass a law. The larger group of politicians is known as the majority, and the smaller group is known as the *minority*. If you are in the minority, you try to encourage members of the majority to change sides.

The legislative branch of our Federal government is called Congress. Congress is made up of the House of Representatives and the Senate. Congress begins its meetings on the third day of January every odd-numbered year. The meetings are called terms and they last two years with a recess, or break, during the summer. The first term of Congress met from 1789-91. The House of Representatives and the Senate meet in different chambers on opposite sides of the Capitol Building in Washington, D.C.

The Congress makes its own rules governing its meetings. It can *expel*, or remove, a member by a two-thirds vote. That means that two thirds of the members, not just a majority, have to agree to an action. A record is kept of all the meetings and is published in the *Congressional Record*.

Members of Congress also have certain

The House of Representatives and the Senate meet in the U.S. Capitol Building.

privileges. They cannot be arrested when going to or coming from Congress, or while attending a session of Congress. A member cannot be sued or punished for anything he or she might say in Congress.

The Constitution goes on to define the individual responsibilities and requirements of the two houses of Congress: the House of Representatives and the Senate, our lawmaking bodies.

THE LEGISLATIVE BRANCH

Introduction
≈ **Challenges** ≈

1. Define:
   Majority: _____

   Minority: _____

   Privilege: _____

   Expel: _____

2. What is the major duty of the legislative branch? _____

   _____

3. What is the legislative body called? _____

   _____

4. Where does it meet? _____

   _____

5. What two houses make up the Congress? _____

   _____

6. When do its meetings begin? _____

   _____

7. What is the name of the record of the meetings of Congress? _____

   _____

8. List two privileges of members of the United States Congress. _____

   _____

   _____

   _____

The House of Representatives
(See Article I, Section 2)

The largest house of Congress is the House of Representatives. There are 435 representatives in the House. The number of representatives a state has is based on the number of people, or population, in the state. There is one representative for every 500,000 people. So if a state has two million people, that state would be able to send four representatives to Washington, D.C.

The term of office for a representative is two years. In order to stay in office, he or she must be reelected every two years.

To find out how many people are in a state, the government conducts a *census*, or count of the people, every ten years. The first census was conducted in 1790. When will the next census occur?

In order to be a representative, there are certain requirements to be met. A representative must be at least 25 years old, must be a citizen of the United States for at least seven years, and must live in the state from which he or she is elected.

The speaker's podium in the House of Representatives' chamber.

Within the House, there are several leaders. The Speaker of the House is the presiding officer. The Speaker is selected by the members of the House and is usually a member of the majority party. The Speaker of the House is second in line to take over the presidency, after the Vice President, in the event of an emergency.

The House of Representatives has the sole power to begin *impeachment* proceedings against a government official. To impeach is to accuse an official of some wrongdoing or misuse of power. The House begins the process by accusing the official, but the trial is carried out by the Senate. More about impeachment will be discussed in later chapters.

Date _____   Name _____

THE LEGISLATIVE BRANCH

The House of Representatives
≈ **Challenges** ≈

1. Define:

    Census: _____

    _____

    Impeach: _____

    _____

2. How many representatives are there in the House of Representatives? _____

3. How many representatives does your state send to Washington, D.C.? _____

4. When was the last census taken in the United States? _____

    When will the next census be taken? _____

5. What was the population of the United States at the last census? _____

6. What are the three qualifications to be a representative?

    a) _____

    b) _____

    c) _____

7. What is the title of the presiding officer of the House? _____

    _____

8. The House begins the impeachment process by doing what? _____

    _____

The Senate
(See Article I, Section 3)

The other house that makes up the Congress is the Senate. The Senate is the smaller of the two groups, with only 100 members. These people are known as senators. Each state, regardless of how big or small, has two senators. Currently there are 50 states, so we have 100 senators in Washington, D.C.

Each senator is elected for a six-year term, but every two years, one third of the senate is up for reelection. For example, in 1992, 33 senators were elected for six-year terms. In 1994, 33 others will be elected, and in 1996, 34 will be elected. This way, there is never an entirely new group of senators; there will always be some experienced senators to guide the newcomers.

According to the original Constitution, the senators were chosen by their state legislatures, but in 1913, the Seventeenth Amendment changed this and allowed the people to elect their senators directly.

In order to be a senator there are certain requirements that must be met. A senator must be at least 30 years old, a citizen of the United States for at least nine years, and live in the state he or she represents.

The Senate also has certain leaders. The Vice President of the United States is in charge of all meetings of the

Senators at their desks in the U.S. Senate chamber.

Senate. He can only vote in the event of a tie between the senators. If the Vice President is absent, the senators choose an alternate presiding officer known as the president pro tempore (temporary president). The president pro tempore is third in line to take over the presidency in the event of an emergency.

With regards to the impeachment process mentioned in the last lesson, the Senate acts as the jury and tries any impeachment cases. When the House of Representatives accuses an official of a crime, the Senate decides whether or not the official is guilty. The Chief Justice of the Supreme Court acts as the judge. Two thirds of the senators present must find the official guilty in order to remove him or her from office.

Date _____   Name _____

THE LEGISLATIVE BRANCH

The Senate

≈ Challenges ≈

1. What are the names of the two houses of Congress? _____

_____

2. How many senators does each state send to Washington? _____

3. What is the total number of senators today? _____

4. What is the term of office of a senator? _____

_____

5. What is the term of office of a representative? _____

_____

6. What are the three requirements to be a senator?

      a) _____

      b) _____

      c) _____

7. What are the titles of the two presiding officers of the Senate? _____

_____

_____

8. What does the Senate do during the impeachment process? _____

_____

_____

Rules, Rights, and Privileges of Congress

(See Article I, Sections 5, 6)

Each house of Congress develops a set of rules for its members, but the Constitution also sets forth specific rules and rights.

In order for a meeting to be held, there must be a *quorum*. A quorum is one person over half of the number of members. For example, for the Senate to have a quorum, there must be 51 senators present (one over half: 51/100). The same is true of the House of Representatives.

The House and Senate may *expel,* or remove, a member for breaking its rules. To expel a member, two thirds of the House or Senate must agree to the removal.

The House and Senate publish the notes, minutes, and records of their meetings in what is known as the *Congressional Record*.

Both houses of Congress must meet in the same city and must meet during the same time. Neither house can *adjourn*, or stop meeting, without the consent of the other house.

Representatives and senators are paid by the United States government, and their salary is set by law. Members of Congress cannot be

Representatives and senators have many duties including meeting with voters, preparing bills and speeches, and attending committee meetings.

arrested during meetings or while going to or from meetings. They also cannot be punished for anything said during one of their meetings.

One right reserved to the House of Representatives is the handling of money matters. Only the House may introduce bills to raise money.

Date _____   Name _____

THE LEGISLATIVE BRANCH
Rules, Rights, and Privileges of Congress
≈ **Challenges** ≈

1. Define:
   Quorum: _____

   _____

   Expel: _____

   _____

   Adjourn: _____

   _____

2. How many representatives from the House of Representatives would need to be present in order for there to be a quorum?

   _____

3. What fraction of the Senate must agree to expel a member? _____

   What number is that? _____

4. Where can you find the notes of the meetings of Congress? _____

   _____

5. Who pays the salaries of representatives and senators? _____

   _____

6. What house is the only house to introduce bills to raise money? _____

   _____

How Bills Become Laws
(See Article I, Section 7)

The laws, or rules, our country has were passed to keep our country functioning. There is a long step-by-step process in the making of laws.

Before a law is a law, it is known as a *bill*. A bill is an idea that a representative or a senator has that he would like to see become a law. A bill may start in either the House of Representatives or the Senate, except for money bills, which must start in the House.

Let's say Senator X has a bill to proclaim June 21 as National Cardinal Day. He takes his bill in written form to his fellow senators, and it is given a code number. If the other senators disagree with the bill, they vote it down, and the bill is dead. If they agree, the bill is passed over to the House of Representatives.

The bill is given to the House of Representatives to discuss and vote on. If they disagree, they vote it down and send it back to the Senate for changes. If the Senate refuses to make changes, the bill dies. If the House approves the bill, it is given to the President for his approval.

If the President agrees with the bill, he signs it and it becomes a law. The

Bills must go through a long, difficult process before they finally become the law of the land.

bill can also become law if the President does not respond to it within ten working days.

If the President does not agree with the bill, he *vetoes* it. With a veto, the President is rejecting the bill. If the President does not sign the bill within ten days after Congress adjourns, the bill dies. This is known as a pocket veto.

If the bill has been vetoed and Congress is still in session, the bill then goes back to the house where it started, in our case, the Senate.

If two thirds of the Senate agree with the bill, that is called *overriding* the President's veto. If the Senate votes to override the veto, then the House of Representatives must override it also. If both houses vote to override the veto, then the bill becomes a law without the President's approval.

Date _____ Name _____

THE LEGISLATIVE BRANCH

How Bills Become Laws
≈ **Challenges** ≈

1. Define:
   Veto: _____

   _____

   Override: _____

   _____

2. Where can a bill be introduced? _____

3. Money bills must be introduced in which house? _____

4. If a bill is approved by the House of Representatives, where must it go next? _____

   _____

5. When both houses approve a bill, then where does it go? _____

   _____

6. If the President vetoes a bill, what process must happen for the bill to become a law?

   _____

   _____

7. What fraction of representatives and senators must agree in order to override the President's veto?

   _____

8. If the veto is not overridden, what happens to the bill? _____

   _____

PROJECT:
Make a bill of your own and explain the process, from beginning to end, of how that bill will become a law.

THE LEGISLATIVE BRANCH

Powers of Congress
(See Article I, Section 8)

The Constitution gives the Congress (the House and the Senate) certain specific powers. Among those listed in Section 8 are the powers to tax, borrow money, regulate commerce (trade), and naturalization (the process by which one can become a United States citizen). Also included are the powers to coin money, establish a system of weights and measurements, establish a post office, declare war, and provide a military. These are many of the important powers specifically granted to the Congress.

Article 1, Section 8, Clause 18 is very important to the Congress. It is known as the "elastic clause." The elastic clause gives Congress the power "to make all laws which shall be necessary and proper" to carry out it's responsibilities.

The powers given to Congress can be broken down into three areas: *enumerated* powers, *implied* powers, and *inherent* powers.

Enumerated powers are powers specifically given to the Congress by the Constitution. They are written. An example would be the power to declare war.

Implied powers are powers given to the Congress that are general. They are stated, but not enough information is given in the Constitution about details. An example would be: the Constitution in Article 1, Section 8, Clause 7 states,

Congress is responsible for maintaining the military forces in the United States.

"To establish post offices and post roads." Obviously, more is needed to run the post office than just roads; there are the mail carriers, security, and buildings. The Constitution assumes that the Congress will take care of these matters, too.

Inherent powers are unlisted powers that a government must have simply because it exists as a government and needs to run its affairs smoothly. The best example of this is the need to conduct foreign affairs. The Constitution does not discuss foreign affairs, but because the United States is a country, we must deal with foreign countries diplomatically.

Date _____ Name _____

THE LEGISLATIVE BRANCH

Powers of Congress
≈ Challenges ≈

1. List and describe four powers given to the Congress by Article I, Section 8:

a) _____

_____

b) _____

_____

c) _____

_____

d) _____

_____

2. What is the "elastic clause"? _____

_____

_____

3. Define enumerated powers and give an example. _____

_____

_____

4. Define implied powers and give an example. _____

_____

_____

5. Define inherent powers and give an example. _____

_____

_____

Limits on Congress and the States

(See Article I, Sections 9, 10)

We saw in the last lesson what powers the Constitution gave the Congress. Now we are going to look at what the Constitution told the Congress it could *not* do.

First, the Constitution told the Congress it could not make any laws outlawing the slave trade until 1808. This clause deals with the rivalry between the northern and southern states. As you will study, this rivalry erupts into the Civil War in 1861.

The second limitation deals with the legal term known as *habeas corpus.* Habeas corpus literally means "you shall have the body." This right of habeas corpus allows a person to be seen and heard in a courtroom by a judge. If you are to be found guilty or not guilty, you have the right to appear in court. The government can not take that right away except in cases of rebellion or invasion.

The Constitution outlawed *bills of attainder.* A bill of attainder is a law passed by the government that convicts a person of a crime and punishes them without a trial.

Another limitation set by the Constitution is that Congress cannot pass *ex post facto laws.* An ex post facto

Prior to the Constitution, people were often arrested and jailed without being charged or having a trial.

law punishes people for a crime that was not a crime when they did it. For example, Mr. Z was smoking a cigarette on his lawn on Monday. On Tuesday, Congress passed a law forbidding smoking in the United States. Wednesday, the police came and arrested Mr. Z for smoking on Monday. When Mr. Z smoked on Monday, it was not a crime. Under the ex post facto clause of the Constitution, punishment of Mr. Z is forbidden.

Other limits on Congress are that it cannot tax products from a state, it cannot give preference to any state's seaport, government money can only be spent by passing a law, and finally, Congress cannot issue titles of nobility. That means the Senate or House cannot make people knights, lords, or duchesses.

The Constitution also puts certain limits on the states. First, they cannot make treaties with other countries. Secondly, they cannot coin their own money. Finally, they cannot do the items mentioned in the above three paragraphs.

The powers of government can be put into three categories: *delegated, concurrent,* and *reserved* powers. Delegated powers are powers that are given to the national government in Washington, D.C., such as the power to declare war. Concurrent powers are powers that are shared between the national and state governments, such as the power to tax. Finally, reserved powers are powers that only the states have, such as the power to create a school system. It is important to keep these different powers in mind as we discuss the remainder of the Constitution.

Date _____   Name _____

THE LEGISLATIVE BRANCH
Limits on Congress and the States
≈ **Challenges** ≈

1. What does "habeas corpus" mean, literally? _____

_____

2. Why does the Constitution prevent Congress from taking away our right of habeas corpus?

_____

_____

3. What is a bill of attainder? _____

_____

4. What is an ex post facto law? Give an example. _____

_____

5. What is one other limit placed on the Congress? _____

_____

6. What are two additional limitations placed on the states by the Constitution?

a) _____

b) _____

7. Explain these three powers:

Delegated: _____

_____

Concurrent: _____

_____

Reserved: _____

_____

THE EXECUTIVE BRANCH

Introduction
(See Article II, Section 1)

As you have seen, the job of the legislative branch is to make the laws. It is the job of the executive branch to carry out, or execute, those laws. They enforce, or make sure people are obeying, the laws made by the legislative branch.

If the Congress makes it a law that the speed limit should be 70 MPH, then it is the job of the executive branch and its offices to make sure that the citizens of the United States are obeying the speed limit.

The executive branch of the United States is very large today. The head of the executive branch is the President, but many thousands of people work for him. The executive branch handles much of the day-to-day work of the country.

The President is the chief executive, and he is elected for a four-year term. His second-in-command is called the Vice President. They are both elected at the same time.

The President and Vice President are chosen by the electoral college. The electoral college is made up of men and women from the different states. Each state gets a certain number of people, or electors. That number is determined by the total number of representatives and senators a state has. For example, if Illinois has 22 representatives and 2 senators, then Illinois would get 24 electors, or people, to vote for the President.

When we go to the polls in a presidential election, our votes are counted and the electors take those totals and elect the President based on who the people have selected. Since the common people were poorly educated and informed in the early years of our nation, the electoral college was originally established to keep the common people from making a mistake and electing a disastrous leader.

If there is a tie in a presidential election, or no one candidate receives a clear majority, then the House of Representatives, with each state having only one vote, elects the President.

The President of the United States lives in the White House.

28

Date _____ Name _____

THE EXECUTIVE BRANCH

Introduction
≈ **Challenges** ≈

1. Define:

  Execute: _____

_____

  Executive: _____

_____

2. If the legislative branch makes the laws, then the executive branch does what with the laws?

_____

3. What is the title of the chief executive, or head, of the executive branch of the United States?

_____

  What is the name of the person who is currently in that office? _____

_____

4. What is the title of the second-in-command? _____

  What is that person's name today? _____

5. What is the job of the electoral college? _____

_____

6. How many electoral votes does your state have today? _____

7. What was the original purpose of the electoral college? _____

_____

8. Who chooses the President in the event of a tie? _____

_____

Qualifications for President

(See Article II, Section 1)

Just as there were requirements to be a representative or a senator, the Constitution set forth certain requirements to be the President of the United States.

In order to be President, a person must be a natural-born citizen of the United States—not an immigrant. He or she must be at least 35 years old and have been a resident of the United States for at least 14 years.

In the event that the President dies or is unfit to continue as President, there is a detailed line of succession. The Vice President assumes the power of the Presidency first; if he is unable, then the Speaker of the House of Representatives takes over. After him is the president pro tempore of the Senate, then the various Cabinet department heads in order of the establishment of the departments, beginning with the Secretary of State. The 25th Amendment outlines what is done when the President dies or is disabled.

The salary of the President is set by the Congress and does not change during the President's term of office. Currently the salary is $200,000.

The President and Vice President are elected on the first Tuesday after the first Monday in November. They are sworn in on Inauguration Day, January 20. Usually, the Chief Justice of the Supreme Court is the person who administers the oath of office to the President at the ceremony. The oath of office is as follows:

"I do solemnly swear (or affirm) that I will faithfully execute the office of President of the United States, and will to the best of my ability, preserve, protect, and defend the Constitution of the United States." "So help me God" is added by the Presidents.

President Bill Clinton taking the oath of office.

THE EXECUTIVE BRANCH

Qualifications for President
≈ **Challenges** ≈

1. What three requirements must be met in order to be President of the United States?

    a) _____

    b) _____

    c) _____

2. In the proper order of succession, who will take over in the event the President dies? List four people.

    a) _____

    b) _____

    c) _____

    d) _____

3. What is the salary of the President?_____

4. When is a President elected? _____

_____

   When is a President inaugurated?_____

_____

   Why do you suppose there is a gap of time? _____

_____

5. Who usually administers the oath of office to the President? _____

_____

Powers and Duties of the President
(See Article II, Section 2.3)

The job of the President is not an easy one. The Constitution spells out many different responsibilities, powers, and duties of the President and the executive branch. The powers of the President can be put into five categories: Commander in Chief, Chief Executive, Chief of State, Chief Legislator, and Chief of Party.

First, the President is the Commander in Chief of the United States Armed Forces. He is the number one military person in the United States. All decisions regarding the Army, Navy, Air Force, and Marines are the responsibility of the President. He can also call the National Guard (or state militias) from the individual states into the service of the United States.

Secondly, the President is the Chief Executive. To run a country the size of the United States, you need many people doing many things. It is the job of the President as Chief Executive to make sure all of his cabinet, staff, and other employees are doing their jobs correctly.

The President is also the Chief of State. This responsibility was given to the President by the Constitution so that the United States would have one person in charge of all foreign relations. The President represents the United States when he or she travels to other countries to meet with foreign leaders. The President also greets and hosts other

The President is the Commander in Chief of the armed forces, and he periodically inspects the troops.

foreign dignitaries when they visit the United States. The President may also make treaties with other countries, but the Senate must ratify, or approve, the treaty by a two-thirds vote.

Another duty of the President is that of Chief Legislator. We saw in Article 1 how the President had the power to veto laws. The Constitution gives the President the power to approve or disapprove of the laws that Congress is making. He can also suggest that certain laws be made by working with his supporters in the House or the Senate.

Finally, the President is also the Chief of Party. When he is elected President, he becomes the head of his political party, Republican or Democratic. He makes decisions regarding the make-up of his individual political party.

Date _____ Name _____

THE EXECUTIVE BRANCH
Powers and Duties of the President
≈ Challenges ≈

1. What are the five categories that the powers of the President can be put into?

a) _____

b) _____

c) _____

d) _____

e) _____

2. What is the President's responsibility to the United States Military? a) What is his title, and b) what can he do?

a) _____

b) _____

_____

3. What is the President's responsibility to the business aspect of the United States government? a) What is his title, and b) what can he do?

a) _____

b) _____

_____

4. What is the President's responsibility to the aspect of foreign relations? a) What is his title, and b) what can he do?

a) _____

b) _____

_____

5. What is the President's responsibility to approve, disapprove, or suggest laws? a) What is his title, and b) what can he do?

a) _____

b) _____

_____

6. What is the President's responsibility to his political party? a) What is his title, and b) what can he do?

a) _____

b) _____

_____

Impeachment

(See Article I, Section 3 and Article II, Section 4)

The Constitution also defines the way to remove officials from office when they have failed at their job. This process is called *impeachment.*

To be removed from office by impeachment, a person must be found guilty of *treason, bribery*, or other high crimes and *misdemeanors*. By high crimes and misdemeanors the founding fathers meant more serious crimes than a traffic ticket.

In order for the impeachment process to begin, the House of Representatives must believe that an official has committed one of the above-mentioned offenses. The House will then come up with a list of charges against the official.

The next step of the process continues in the Senate. The senators act as the jury and hear both sides of the case against the accused official. When it is the President being tried, the Chief Justice of the Supreme Court acts as the judge. Two thirds of the Senate must agree in order for the official to be convicted of the charges and removed from office.

In all of United States history, no President has ever been removed from office by impeachment. Two Presidents, however, have gone through part or all of the impeachment process.

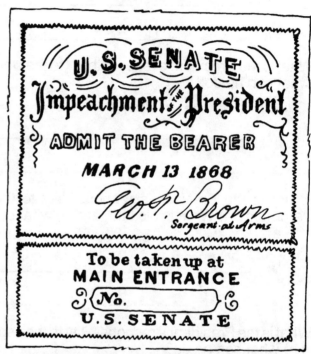

During the impeachment of President Andrew Johnson, tickets were issued to the public for admittance to the trial.

In 1867, President Andrew Johnson was charged with several offenses, and the House voted to impeach him. The Senate held the trial, and when the vote was taken, Johnson escaped being convicted by only one vote!

In 1974, the House of Representatives began to investigate President Richard Nixon and his involvement with the break-in of the Watergate Office Complex in Washington, D.C. By the end of July, 1974, the House had prepared several charges against President Nixon. Instead of letting the impeachment process go any further, Nixon resigned as President on August 9, 1974. Nixon was the first President ever to resign.

THE EXECUTIVE BRANCH

Impeachment
≈ Challenges ≈

1. Define:
   Impeach: _____

_____

   Misdemeanor: _____

_____

   Bribery: _____

_____

   Treason: _____

_____

2. Which house of Congress begins the impeachment process? _____

_____

3. Which house of Congress acts as the jury and tries the case? _____

_____

4. Who acts as the judge at the impeachment trial of a President? _____

_____

5. In order for an official to be convicted, what fraction of the Senate needs to agree?

_____

6. Who was the only President to have gone through the entire impeachment process? When?

_____

7. At what point during the impeachment process did President Nixon resign? When?

_____

8. How many Presidents have been removed from office by being found guilty after the impeachment process?

_____

Organization of the Executive Branch and the Cabinet
(See Article II, Section 2.3)

As we have seen, the executive branch of the United States government is quite large. Let's look now at what makes up the executive branch and the Cabinet.

There are four divisions of the executive branch: the Cabinet departments, independent agencies, government corporations, and regulatory agencies.

While the Constitution did not specifically create the Cabinet, President Washington in 1789 felt he needed advisors. The Cabinet is a group of men and women who are the President's closest advisors. They are each in charge of one of the fourteen departments. A list of the Cabinet Departments may be found on page 66 of this workbook. The most important Cabinet departments are the Department of State, Department of Defense, and the Department of the Treasury. Each advisor is given the title of "Secretary." If you were head of the Department of State, for example, you would be known as the Secretary of State. Each department head, or secretary, has many people working under him or her to keep the government running smoothly. Each Cabinet department deals with specific areas of national concern.

The Cabinet meeting room.

Another section of the executive branch overseen by the President is the independent agencies. These agencies are not as important as Cabinet departments, but are essential to the mission of the United States. One example of an independent agency is the National Aeronautics and Space Administration (NASA).

A third category is known as government corporations. These are businesses run by the United States government in order to provide specific services to the people. The United States Postal Service is a government corporation. Another example is the Federal Deposit Insurance Corporation (FDIC), which insures the money that is deposited in banks.

The final division of the executive branch is the regulatory commissions. These groups make sure that the rules set for certain large industries are being followed and that the safety of the public is not in jeopardy. Examples are the Federal Communications Commission (FCC), which licenses radio and television stations, and the Federal Aviation Administration (FAA), which makes sure airports, aircraft, and pilots are safe.

As you can see, the President has a great deal of responsibility and a large number of people to oversee to ensure that the government is functioning properly.

Date _____ Name _____

THE EXECUTIVE BRANCH
Organization of the Executive Branch and the Cabinet
≈ Challenges ≈

1. What are the four divisions of the executive branch?

   a) _____

   b) _____

   c) _____

   d) _____

2. How many cabinet departments are there? _____

3. What is the title of the head of the Department of Defense? _____

_____

4. Referring to page 66, list three more cabinet departments.

   a) _____

   b) _____

   c) _____

5. Which President created the Cabinet? When? _____

_____

6. Give an example of an independent agency. _____

_____

7. Give an example of a government corporation. _____

_____

8. Give an example of a regulatory commission. _____

_____

DEBATE: *What are the pros and cons of having a national executive?*

THE JUDICIAL BRANCH AND ARTICLES IV-VII

Organization of the Judicial Branch
(See Article III, Section 1)

The third branch of the United States government is the judicial branch. We learned that the legislative branch makes the laws and that the executive branch carries out and enforces the laws. It is the job of the judicial branch to interpret, or explain, the laws.

When Congress passes a law, and the President enforces it, it is then the job of the Supreme Court to decide what those laws really mean. The Supreme Court is the major body of the judicial branch. The Supreme Court Building is located in Washington, D.C. The Supreme Court is the highest, and most important, court in the United States. The Constitution spells out what kinds of cases it can hear and what the powers of the Court are. The Constitution also provides for lower courts as well.

The Supreme Court is made up of nine justices, or judges. There are eight associate justices and one chief justice. The justices are appointed by the President and are approved by the Senate. Once approved, they serve for life. They cannot be removed except by impeachment. When deciding a case, only five of the nine must agree to reach a decision. The salaries of the justices cannot be lowered during their time in office. With these checks and balances, the judicial branch is free from interference by the other branches.

There are several other court systems under the Supreme Court. The lowest Federal courts under the judicial system are the district courts. There are 91 district courts in the United States. After a case has been heard in the district court, it moves to the United States Court of Appeals. It is here where a case can be appealed, or heard for a second time, to reverse the original judgment. There are 12 appeals courts.

There are also several other courts that feed into the Supreme Court. The highest court in any state is usually the state supreme court. A case can be appealed from a state supreme court to the United States Supreme Court. The Court of Military Appeals, the United States Tax Court, and the United States Claims Court also feed cases to the Supreme Court. These courts hear specialized cases.

The Supreme Court Building

Date_____ Name _____

THE JUDICIAL BRANCH AND ARTICLES IV-VII
Organization of the Judicial Branch
≈ **Challenges** ≈

1. Define:
   Judicial: _____

   _____

   Appeal: _____

   _____

2. What is the job of the judicial branch? _____

   _____

. . . legislative branch?_____

   _____

. . . executive branch?_____

   _____

3. What is the name of the highest, most important court in the United States? _____

   _____

4. What are the titles of the men and women who serve on the high court? _____

   _____

5. How many serve on the high court? _____ How long do they serve? _____

   _____

6. Who appoints the justices, and who must approve of them?_____

   _____

7. There are 91_____ courts and 12 _____ courts that report to
   the Supreme Court.

8. Name two other courts that are part of the Federal judicial system._____

   _____

Cases for the Supreme Court
(See Article III, Section 2)

The Constitution tells the Federal courts exactly what types of cases they can hear. The Supreme Court only has the jurisdiction, or power to hear cases, that the Constitution gives it. For example, the Supreme Court does not handle divorce cases, but the Constitution says the Court may hear cases involving two or more individual state governments.

The kinds of cases the Federal and Supreme Courts may hear are cases coming from any question involving: 1) the Constitution, 2) Federal laws, 3) treaties, and 4) laws governing ships. The courts may also hear cases coming from people concerning: 1) ambassadors or public ministers, 2) the United States government itself, 3) two or more state governments, 4) citizens of different states, and 5) a state or its citizens versus a foreign country or foreign citizen.

These cases are what are known as *original jurisdiction.* Under *appellate jurisdiction,* the Supreme Court can only hear a case after it has gone through the court system first (the district courts and the appeals courts, or the state supreme court). Only after these lower courts have heard the case can the Supreme Court respond.

If a case has made it through the court system and wishes to be heard by the Supreme Court, the lawyers must submit to the nine justices what is called a *writ of certiorari* (cert). A writ of cert is a formal request to the Supreme Court to hear a case. The justices vote and either accept or reject that request based upon the possible impact of the case on society, or simply because of the large number of cases they have to hear. If a case is decided by the Supreme Court, it has traveled a long way to get there!

There are eight associate justices and one chief justice on the Supreme Court.

THE JUDICIAL BRANCH AND ARTICLES IV-VIII
Cases for the Supreme Court
≈ Challenges ≈

1. Define:
   Jurisdiction: _____

_____

2. List nine types of cases the Supreme and Federal Courts have jurisdiction over:

   a) _____

   b) _____

   c) _____

   d) _____

   e) _____

   f) _____

   g) _____

   h) _____

   i) _____

3. What is original jurisdiction? _____

_____

4. What is appellate jurisdiction? _____

_____

5. What is a writ of certiorari? _____

_____

PROJECT:
  Take a case beginning in the United States District Court and trace it to the Supreme Court.

Judicial Review and Treason
(See Article III, Section 3)

There are two important legal concepts that need to be discussed at this point, the first of which is called judicial review.

We saw in the last lesson what types of powers the Supreme Court has. In 1803, in a case before the Supreme Court, another important power of the Supreme Court was begun. That was the power to declare a law *unconstitutional,* meaning the law goes against the Constitution of the United States.

For example, we know the Constitution states that there should be two senators from each state. If Congress passed a law saying there should only be one senator from a state, the Supreme Court could look at that law and declare it unconstitutional. That means Congress's law is void because the Constitution is more important and is the supreme law of the land. This process of checking the laws is known as *judicial review.* The job of the Supreme Court is to review the laws of our country.

Another concept mentioned by the Constitution is that of *treason.* Treason is defined as carrying on war against the United States and giving help to the nation's enemies. Treason is a very serious crime, and it is one of the charges that may be involved in the impeachment process. In order to be convicted of treason, two witnesses must testify to the same story, and/or the accused must make a confession in a courtroom.

John Marshall, chief justice from 1801 to 1835, was responsible for broadening the powers of the Supreme Court, especially the power of judicial review.

To quickly review, we've seen the three branches of our Federal government. The legislative branch makes our laws, the executive branch carries out our laws, and the judicial branch defines our laws. There are many people who make our laws and help run our country, just as there are many who defend our rights and freedoms as Americans.

THE JUDICIAL BRANCH AND ARTICLES IV-VII
Judicial Review and Treason
≈ Challenges ≈

1. Define:

    Unconstitutional: _____

_____

    Treason: _____

_____

2. The process of checking the laws of our land is called: _____

_____

3. What does it mean when the Supreme Court declares a law "unconstitutional"?

_____

4. Give an example of an act of treason. _____

_____

5. What must happen in court for a person to be convicted of treason? _____

_____

_____

6. What does the executive branch do? _____

_____

7. What does the judicial branch do? _____

_____

8. What does the legislative branch do? _____

_____

Article IV: The States

(See Article IV, Sections 1-4)

In the first three Articles of the Constitution, the founding fathers established the physical structure of our government. But there were still other issues to be solved before the Constitution could begin its work.

The issues still remaining involved the roles of the states in the new government, how to make changes to the Constitution, and how to get the Constitution approved by the current states.

First, in Article IV, the Constitution addresses the states. Before the Constitution, each state acted individually on many issues. It was like having 13 separate countries with a mediocre friendship. The Articles of Confederation had supported this loose association of states. But by 1787, as we studied earlier, the loose friendship was in trouble.

The Constitution set forth a strong central government. The states were not going to be happy with giving up many of the rights they exercised during the previous years. So, the framers of the Constitution wrote Article IV.

The relationships between the individual states had been tense, so Article IV demanded that each state respect the laws and decisions of the other states. Each state is required to treat citizens of the other states the

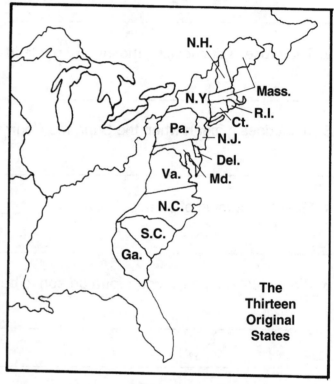

The Thirteen Original States

Article IV deals with the relationships between the states.

same way it would treat one of its own citizens. If a person broke a law in Missouri and escaped to Georgia, Georgia would be required to send the criminal back to Missouri. The states must work together and respect each other.

Article IV also provides a way for new states to be admitted into the union. Congress was given the power to admit new states, but no new state could come from the property of an existing state, and no two states could join together to form a larger one, unless both state legislatures and Congress approved.

Finally, Article IV guarantees each state a *republican* form of government. What this means is that each state will always have a government elected by the people and not a monarchy. The Federal government will also defend the states against invasion or attack because the states will no longer have individual militaries.

THE JUDICIAL BRANCH AND ARTICLES IV-VII
Article IV: The States
≈ **Challenges** ≈

1. Define:
    Republican: _____

_____

2. What issue does Article IV address? _____

_____

3. What must the state of Oregon do about the laws of Idaho? _____

_____

4. Who is given the power to admit new states? _____

5. Could Rhode Island, Vermont, and New Hampshire join together to form a new state? How?

_____

_____

6. What is a republican form of government? _____

_____

_____

7. Under the Articles of Confederation, how could the relationship between the states be described?

_____

_____

_____

8. Under the Constitution, how could the new relationship between the states be described?

_____

_____

_____

Amending the Constitution

(See Article V)

When the founding fathers were writing the Constitution in 1787, they were thinking far into the future. If the Constitution was to become a lasting part of American government, there would have to be room for change. Article V is perhaps the most important part of the Constitution.

Article V provides a way for the Constitution to be *amended,* or changed. The process by which the Constitution can be changed is not an easy one. There are many steps that must be gone through. By making the process a difficult one, the framers hoped to avoid changing the Constitution too quickly. Any change that would be made must be a good one.

There are two ways to propose an amendment to the Constitution. For example, let's say we wish to lower the age requirement to be President from 35 to 30. One way to start the amendment would be to get two thirds of both houses of Congress (House and Senate) to agree. The other way to propose an amendment is through a constitutional convention called by two thirds of the state legislatures.

If our amendment was approved by either of the two above groups, then the amendment must be *ratified,* or formally approved. There are two ways to ratify an amendment: three fourths of the legislatures in the states must ratify

Parades were held to encourage the passage of the Nineteenth Amendment, which granted suffrage to women.

any amendment, or three fourths of the states must have individual constitutional conventions to ratify the amendment.

Throughout the past 200-plus years, there have only been 27 changes to the structure of the Constitution. Our founding fathers established a system that was basically sound and problem free. While there are, of course, errors, the United States Constitution is the oldest written constitution in the world. Our Constitution has been the example that many other countries of the world have used to formulate their own governments. We can be proud of that!

Date _____ Name _____

THE JUDICIAL BRANCH AND ARTICLES IV-VII
Amending the Constitution
≈ Challenges ≈

1. Define:

    Amend: _____

    _____

    Ratify: _____

    _____

2. What issue does Article V address?_____

    _____

3. What two ways can an amendment be proposed?

    a) _____

    _____

    b) _____

    _____

4. What two ways can an amendment be ratified?

    a) _____

    _____

    b) _____

    _____

5. What fraction must propose an amendment, and what fraction must ratify an amendment?

    _____

    _____

Articles VI and VII
(See Articles VI and VII)

Articles VI and VII complete the original Constitution. Article VI confirms the authority of the Constitution, and Article VII describes how the Constitution must be ratified, or approved.

In Article VI, the founding fathers establish the Constitution as the "supreme law of the land." The Constitution is the highest, most important document in the United States. No state, county, or city laws will be superior to the Constitution. It is the job of the judicial branch to see that no laws in the country are in conflict with the Constitution. For example, if Indiana passed a law making it possible for Indiana to print its own money, that law would be void, or unenforceable, because the Constitution says that only the Congress can print or coin money. Article VI also states that officials of the United States government must promise to support the Constitution.

The signing of the Constitution

Article VII is the final section of the original Constitution. When the Constitution was written during the summer of 1787, the Articles of Confederation were still governing the United States. In order for the Articles to be replaced by the Constitution, the Constitution had to be ratified, or approved, by nine states. So in order for the plan of government set forth in the Constitution to begin, nine of the thirteen states had to approve. They completed the Constitution on September 17, 1787, twelve years after the United States declared its independence from England.

The writers of the Constitution then signed the document. Their names are below:

George Washington, Virginia
President of the Convention

Delaware:	George Read, Gunning Bedford, Jr., John Dickinson, Richard Bassett, Jacob Broom
Maryland:	James McHenry, Daniel of St. Thomas Jenifer, Daniel Carroll
Virginia:	John Blair, James Madison, Jr.
North Carolina:	William Blount, Richard Dobbs Spaight, Hugh Williamson
South Carolina:	John Rutledge, Charles Cotesworth Pinckney, Charles Pinckney, Pierce Butler
Georgia:	William Few, Abraham Baldwin
New Hampshire:	John Langdon, Nicholas Gilman
Massachusetts:	Nathanial Gorman, Rufus King
Connecticut:	William Samuel Johnson, Roger Sherman
New York:	Alexander Hamilton
New Jersey:	William Livingston, David Brearley, William Paterson, Jonathon Dayton
Pennsylvania:	Benjamin Franklin, Thomas Mifflin, Robert Morris, George Clymer, Thomas FitzSimons, Jared Ingersoll, James Wilson, Gouverneur Morris

THE JUDICIAL BRANCH AND ARTICLES IV-VII
Articles VI and VII
≈ **Challenges** ≈

1. Why did the framers include Article VI in the Constitution? _____

_____

_____

2. Is it possible for the city of Chicago to make a treaty with the country of Germany? Why or why not?

_____

_____

3. How many states must ratify the Constitution before it can go into effect? _____

4. On what day was the Constitution signed? _____

5. How many years after the Declaration of Independence was the Constitution written?

_____

6. What document was governing the United States before and during the writing of the Constitution?

_____

7. List four signers of the Constitution whose names you recognize:

a) _____

b) _____

c) _____

d) _____

THE AMENDMENTS

Introduction

As you studied earlier, the path to amending the Constitution is a difficult one. Throughout the past 200 years, many, many amendments have been suggested in Congress. Of those, only 27 amendments have become part of the Constitution.

The contents of the amendments are very different. The first amendments deal with rights that many felt should have been included in the main body of the Constitution. These first ten amendments are called the Bill of Rights. Other amendments deal with changes in American society over the years, such as slavery and prohibition. Finally, other amendments change sections of the Constitution.

The Constitution, the Bill of Rights, and the Declaration of Independence are on display at the National Archives in Washington, D.C.

Below is a chart briefly describing the Amendments:

Amendment	Year Ratified	Description
I	1791	Freedom of religion, press, speech, assembly, petition
II	1791	Right to bear arms
III	1791	Quartering of soldiers
IV	1791	Unreasonable searches and seizures
V	1791	Right of due process of law, no double jeopardy
VI	1791	Right to a public trial, right to a lawyer
VII	1791	Right to a jury trial
VIII	1791	Excessive bail, no cruel and unusual punishment
IX	1791	Rights not listed in the Constitution
X	1791	Rights to the people and states
XI	1798	Lawsuits against states
XII	1804	Presidential/Vice Presidential elections
XIII	1865	Abolition of Slavery
XIV	1868	Former slaves granted citizenship
XV	1870	Black suffrage
XVI	1913	Income tax
XVII	1913	Direct election of senators
XVIII	1919	Prohibition of alcoholic beverages
XIX	1920	Women's suffrage
XX	1933	Lame duck period
XXI	1933	Repeal of prohibition
XXII	1951	Limit of two terms as President
XXIII	1961	Suffrage for District of Columbia
XXIV	1964	Abolition of poll taxes
XXV	1967	Presidential succession
XXVI	1971	Eighteen-year-old vote
XXVII	1992	Limits on Congressional pay raises

Date _____ Name _____

THE AMENDMENTS

Introduction
≈ **Challenges** ≈

1. How many amendments have been added to the Constitution? _____

_____

2. What are the first ten amendments called? _____

_____

3. In what year were the first ten amendments added? _____

_____

4. When was the most recent amendment and what was it? _____

_____

5. Which amendment abolished slavery? When? _____

_____

6. What did the 19th Amendment in 1920 give to women? _____

_____

7. Under which amendment are we guaranteed the freedom of religion? _____

_____

8. Why have there been amendments to the Constitution? _____

_____

_____

_____

PROJECT:
Select an article or amendment from the Constitution and paraphrase it (write it in your own words).

The Bill of Rights, 1791: Amendments I-III

(See Amendments I-III)

In 1791, two years after the Constitution went into effect, ten amendments were added to the document. It was felt that the Constitution did not list the rights that should be protected for all Americans. The Constitution assumed that because the powers of the government were specific and limited, a statement of rights was not needed. As the states began to ratify the Constitution in 1787 and 1788, they insisted that a Bill of Rights be added.

The first three amendments guarantee certain individual freedoms that today we cherish as Americans. The First Amendment gives Americans the freedom to choose their own religion. Congress cannot pass a law making any religion the official religion of the United States. Under the First Amendment we are also given the freedom of *speech* (the right to speak out without fear of punishment), freedom of the *press* (the right of newspapers to print whatever they feel is newsworthy without censorship), freedom of *assembly* (the right to gather together in a group), and the right of *petition* (the right to ask the government to change things). People are guaranteed these freedoms so far as they do not take away the freedoms of others. It is the job of the courts to decide where that line is drawn. These basic freedoms have been the subject of many court cases throughout the history of the United States.

The Bill of Rights was ratified in 1791.

The Second Amendment gives American citizens the right to bear *arms*. Arms are weapons or guns. Under this amendment, Americans are allowed to own guns. There is much controversy today surrounding this amendment. What types of weapons should we be allowed to own and use for protection or hunting?

The Third Amendment had its beginning during the French and Indian War and the Revolutionary War. It outlaws the *quartering*, or housing, of soldiers in private houses. Before independence, English soldiers would forcibly move into the homes of Americans. The Third Amendment prohibits this practice in peacetime and authorizes Congress to pass a law concerning quartering of soldiers in wartime.

Date _____ Name _____

THE AMENDMENTS
The Bill of Rights, 1791: Amendments I-III
≈ **Challenges** ≈

1. Define:

    Assembly: _____

_____

    Petition: _____

_____

    Quartering: _____

_____

2. Why did Americans insist on adding the Bill of Rights to the Constitution? _____

_____

3. What five freedoms does the First Amendment guarantee?

    a) _____

    b) _____

    c) _____

    d) _____

    e) _____

4. What does the Second Amendment guarantee? _____

_____

5. What does the Third Amendment prohibit? _____

_____

6. The First Amendment guarantees us freedom of speech. Do you think it's okay to scream "Fire!" in a crowded theater when there is no fire? Why or why not?

_____

_____

The Bill of Rights, 1791: Amendments IV-VI
(See Amendments IV, V, VI)

The Fourth Amendment is concerned with searches and seizures. In order to convict a person of a crime, you need to have evidence. Where is the best place to find evidence but in the home or on the person? Before the Constitution, there was no protection against the police or government invading your home or arresting you at any time. The Fourth Amendment outlaws unreasonable searches and seizures. The government must have a *search warrant* in order to search your home. A search warrant is a document issued by a judge to the sheriff for the purpose of getting evidence concerning a crime. An *arrest warrant* is similar, but for the purpose of arresting someone suspected of a crime. The Fourth Amendment protects us from being wrongly arrested or searched.

The Fifth Amendment gives Americans many basic legal protections. First, no one can be tried for a serious crime without an indictment by a *grand jury*. A grand jury is a group of people who decide if there is enough evidence to have a trial. If there is enough evidence, they issue an *indictment*, which is a formal charge, or accusation, against a person.

The Fifth Amendment also protects against *double jeopardy*. Double jeopardy is when a person is tried twice for the same crime. The Fifth Amendment says that once a person has gone

The Fourth, Fifth, and Sixth Amendments protect those accused of crimes.

through a trial and been found innocent, there cannot be another trial later, even if more evidence is found. The government also cannot punish a person twice for one crime. The amendment also protects people from having to witness against themselves. This is called *self-incrimination.*

Also guaranteed by the Fifth Amendment is the right to *due process of law.* Whatever the government does, it cannot take away someone's life, liberty, or property without first going through the proper steps set forth in our laws. Finally, if the government takes property, the owner must be paid a fair price.

In the Sixth Amendment, we are guaranteed the right to a fair, fast, and public trial. People who are accused of a crime also have the right to be present in court and have a lawyer represent them, even if they cannot afford one. The Sixth Amendment protects the rights of the accused.

Date _____   Name _____

THE AMENDMENTS
The Bill of Rights, 1791: Amendments IV-VI
≈ **Challenges** ≈

1. What is a search warrant? _____

_____

2. What is an arrest warrant? _____

_____

3. What is a grand jury? _____

_____

4. What is an indictment? _____

_____

5. What is double jeopardy? _____

_____

6. What amendment guarantees the right of due process of the law? _____

_____

7. Which amendment protects people from unreasonable searches and seizures? _____

_____

8. Which amendment protects people from being tried twice for the same crime? _____

_____

9. Which amendment guarantees the right to a lawyer, even if a person can't afford one?

_____

10. Which amendment prevents the courts from forcing a person to witness against himself?

_____

The Bill of Rights, 1791: Amendments VII-X

(See Amendments VII, VIII, IX, X)

The final section of the Bill of Rights deals with legal rights and also with powers given to the states.

The Seventh Amendment guarantees Americans the right to a trial by a jury in any case involving more than twenty dollars. In today's society there are many lawsuits going through the court system. It is our right to have our case decided by a group of our peers, a *jury.* Or, it is our right to not have a jury and have only a judge decide the case.

The Eighth Amendment protects us from having to pay excessive *bail* or be punished in cruel and unusual ways. Bail is money that is given in order to be released from jail. The money is returned when the accused appears in court for the trial. Protection from paying excessive bail means that one wouldn't have to pay one million dollars to be released from jail for stealing a candy bar! Cruel and unusual punishment is being tortured or punished in ways that are not humane. There are many different opinions as to what is cruel and unusual punishment.

The Seventh Amendment guarantees the right to a trial by jury.

The Ninth Amendment is the "etcetera" amendment. Under this amendment, other rights not listed in the Constitution are also given to the people. The rights in the Constitution are not the only rights Americans have—they are just a few. The Ninth Amendment protects other rights that might not have been listed.

Finally, the Tenth Amendment gives all powers not specifically listed in the Constitution to the states and its peoples. For example, education is not mentioned in the Constitution; therefore, it is the job of the individual states to educate its people. What is not written in the Constitution is given to the states and the people.

The Bill of Rights is an important addition to the Constitution. Without the statement of these rights, certain freedoms like religion, speech, or public trials might have been lost in the passage of time.

THE AMENDMENTS
The Bill of Rights, 1791: Amendments VII-X
≈ **Challenges** ≈

1. What is a jury? _____

_____

2. What does the Seventh Amendment guarantee? _____

_____

_____

3. What is excessive bail? _____

_____

4. What would you consider cruel and unusual punishment? _____

_____

5. What does the Eighth Amendment protect us from? _____

_____

_____

6. What does the Ninth Amendment say about rights not listed in the Constitution?

_____

_____

7. The power to set up school districts is not stated in the Constitution. Who has the authority to create schools?

_____

   What amendment gives them that power? _____

8. How many amendments are contained in the Bill of Rights? _____

_____

THE AMENDMENTS

1798-1870: Amendments XI-XV
(See Amendments XI, XII, XIII, XIV, XV)

After the Bill of Rights became part of the Constitution, other changes were made by other amendments.

The Eleventh Amendment was added to the Constitution in 1798. Under the amendment, people in one state, or foreigners, cannot sue another state in a Federal court.

The Twelfth Amendment, concerning presidential elections, was ratified in 1804. Before the Twelfth Amendment, the man who received the most votes was the President, and the man with the second most votes was the Vice President. But by the election of 1800, political parties had developed, and it was clear that having two men from different parties was not a good leadership situation. The Twelfth Amendment allowed voters to vote for the President and Vice President on separate ballots so that members of the same political party would not be running against each other for the presidency.

The Thirteenth Amendment was a result of the Civil War. Passed in 1865, the Thirteenth Amendment abolished slavery. Slavery had been a part of the United States since the 1600s, and it took a civil war to end the practice.

The Fourteenth Amendment, ratified in 1868, was part of the Reconstruction Era. Under this

The Fifteenth Amendment gave blacks the right to vote.

amendment, all Americans, regardless of race, were guaranteed the rights listed in the Constitution. This amendment also included blacks in population counts for the census. Finally, the Fourteenth Amendment prohibited Confederate officers from holding government positions and refused to pay Confederate war debts or reimburse owners for their now-freed slaves.

Finally, the Fifteenth Amendment, ratified in 1870, gave blacks *suffrage*, or the right to vote. Before 1870, many states had prohibited blacks from voting. But with the end of the Civil War and the passage of the Fourteenth Amendment, the next step was to give black males the right to vote.

Between 1791 and 1870—eighty years—only five changes had been made to the Constitution. In the next lesson you will study the changes made from 1900 to 1950.

58

Date _____   Name _____

THE AMENDMENTS

1798-1870: Amendments XI-XV
≈ **Challenges** ≈

1. In what years were the following amendments ratified?

     a) Amendment XI   _____

     b) Amendment XII   _____

     c) Amendment XIII   _____

     d) Amendment XIV   _____

     e) Amendment XV   _____

2. How does the Twelfth Amendment change how the President and Vice President are elected?

_____

_____

3. What war was the Thirteenth Amendment a result of? _____

_____

4. What does the Thirteenth Amendment abolish? _____

_____

5. Under the Fourteenth Amendment, who is guaranteed the rights listed in the Constitution?

_____

6. What is suffrage? _____

7. Who was given suffrage with the Fifteenth Amendment? _____

_____

8. Between what years were the Eleventh to Fifteenth Amendments ratified? —————

_____

1900-1950: Amendments XVI-XXI
(See Amendments XVI, XVII, XVIII, XIX, XX, XXI)

This next group of amendments was ratified during the first half of the 1900s. This group of amendments also made specific changes to the American system.

The Sixteenth Amendment, ratified in 1913, gave Congress the power to establish an income tax. Before 1913, the only way the government made money was through *tariffs* (taxes on imports). With the Sixteenth Amendment, the government could now tax people's incomes. Each person was taxed according to the amount of money he or she made.

Also in 1913, the Seventeenth Amendment was added to the Constitution changing the way senators were elected. Article I of the Constitution stated that the senators were to be elected by the state legislatures. The Seventeenth Amendment allowed the American people to directly elect their senators, just like other elected officials.

During the first two decades of the twentieth century, a movement in the United States to ban the use of alcohol was gaining strength. Many people saw the "evils of drinking" and felt that the production, sale, and use

Government agents destroyed alcohol outlawed by the Eighteenth Amendment.

of alcoholic beverages should be prohibited. So, in 1919, the Eighteenth Amendment was ratified, and the United States entered the *Prohibition* Era.

Another reform movement sweeping the United States during this time concerned women and their right to vote. Previously, American women were not given the right to vote. The Fifteenth Amendment had given black males the right to vote. Women's groups had been fighting since the mid-1800s for suffrage, or the right to vote. In 1920, with the ratification of the Nineteenth Amendment, women were given the right to vote.

The Twentieth Amendment, passed in 1933, changed the dates when elected officials took office. In 1787 when the Constitution was written, travel was very slow, and news traveled even slower. Because of this, the President and Congress were given many months between their elections and the time when they were sworn in. The old officials were known as "lame ducks" because they did not have much time or power left. This amendment shortened the President's "lame duck" period from March 4 to January 20. Congress begins its terms and meetings on January 3.

Finally, also in 1933, the Twenty-first Amendment was passed repealing the Eighteenth Amendment. This amendment ended the Prohibition Era. The Eighteenth Amendment failed because of a lack of enforcement, and too many Americans were opposed to Prohibition.

Date _____   Name _____

THE AMENDMENTS
1900-1950: Amendments XVI-XXI
≈ **Challenges** ≈

1. Define:
   Prohibition: _____

_____

2. In what years were the following amendments ratified?

   a) Amendment XVI   _____

   b) Amendment XVII   _____

   c) Amendment XVIII   _____

   d) Amendment XIX   _____

   e) Amendment XX   _____

   f) Amendment XXI   _____

3. The Sixteenth Amendment gave Congress the power to _____

_____

4. Who elected the senators before the Seventeenth Amendment? _____

_____

   Who elects our senators now? _____

5. Why did many Americans support the Eighteenth Amendment? _____

_____

6. Which amendment repealed the Eighteenth Amendment? _____

7. Which group of Americans was given suffrage with the Nineteenth Amendment?

_____

8. What does the Twentieth Amendment change? Why? _____

_____

1950-Present: Amendments XXII-XXVII
(See Amendments XXII, XXIII, XXIV, XXV, XXVI, XXVII)

This final group of amendments focuses on the President and other American civil rights.

The Twenty-second Amendment, ratified in 1951, limited the amount of terms a President could serve. The Constitution did not put a limit on the number of terms a President could serve. President George Washington had only served two terms, or eight years. Because of his example, or precedent, other presidents only served a maximum of two terms. This changed when Franklin D. Roosevelt was elected to a third term in 1940, and a fourth term in 1944. The Twenty-second Amendment limited the President to two terms of office.

The Twenty-sixth Amendment made it possible for those eighteen years old to vote.

Before 1961, citizens of the District of Columbia had no voice in elections, and by the 1960s, the District had a large population that was left out. The Twenty-third Amendment, passed in 1961, gave citizens who lived in the District of Columbia the right to vote in national elections.

In 1964, the Twenty-fourth Amendment was added to the Constitution. Before this amendment, many states would place a tax on voting. In order to vote in an election, you would be forced to pay a poll tax. This amendment prohibited the poll tax.

With the assassination of President Kennedy on November 22, 1963, the nation was made more aware of who takes over in the event of an emergency. Lyndon Johnson, Kennedy's Vice President, took over as President, but there was no Vice President to take over in the event Johnson died. The Twenty-fifth Amendment, passed in 1967, allowed the new President to appoint a Vice President. The Congress would have to approve of this new Vice President by a majority vote of both houses. If a President becomes ill, he may temporarily give his powers to the Vice President until he has recovered. This amendment was used in 1973 and 1974 with the resignations of Vice President Agnew and President Nixon. Nixon appointed Gerald Ford to replace Agnew in 1973, then Ford became President in 1974 when Nixon resigned, and he appointed Nelson Rockefeller to be Vice President.

The Twenty-sixth Amendment, ratified in 1971, was aimed at the young people of the United States. Many Americans felt that the voting age should be lowered from 21 to 18. So, in 1971, 18-year-olds were given the right to vote.

The final amendment to the United States Constitution was ratified on May 7, 1992. The Twenty-seventh Amendment tells senators and representatives that any changes in their salaries will not take effect until after the next election. This amendment was originally part of the Bill of Rights of 1789, but was not ratified along with the others. It was not until 1992 that it became part of the Constitution!

Date _____   Name _____

THE AMENDMENTS

1950-Present: Amendments XXII-XXVII
≈ **Challenges** ≈

1. In what years were the following amendments ratified?

    a) Amendment XXII   _____

    b) Amendment XXIII   _____

    c) Amendment XXIV   _____

    d) Amendment XXV   _____

    e) Amendment XXVI   _____

    f) Amendment XXVII   _____

2. According to the Twenty-second Amendment, for how many terms can one be elected as President?

_____

3. Who was given the right to vote by the Twenty-third Amendment? _____

_____

4. What group was given suffrage with the Twenty-sixth Amendment? _____

_____

5. What practice was outlawed by the Twenty-fourth Amendment? _____

_____

6. If a President dies and the Vice President takes over, what must happen to get a new Vice President?

_____

7. What amendment authorizes the above situation? _____

8. What does the Twenty-seventh Amendment say about the salaries of senators and representatives?

_____

9. How long has it taken the Twenty-seventh Amendment to be ratified? _____

Activity One: The United States in Ratification Order

DIRECTIONS: Using a history book, almanac, or encyclopedia, find the order in which the states entered the United States. Find the date when each state entered, and list them in the proper order. The first one is done for you.

NO.	STATE	DATE
1	Delaware	December 7, 1787

CONTINUE ON THE BACK OF THIS SHEET

Activity Two: Presidents of the United States

DIRECTIONS: Using a history book or an encyclopedia, list the Presidents of the United States from first to last. The first one is done for you.

1. George Washington _____   22. _____

2. _____   23. _____

3. _____   24. _____

4. _____   25. _____

5. _____   26. _____

6. _____   27. _____

7. _____   28. _____

8. _____   29. _____

9. _____   30. _____

10. _____   31. _____

11. _____   32. _____

12. _____   33. _____

13. _____   34. _____

14. _____   35. _____

15. _____   36. _____

16. _____   37. _____

17. _____   38. _____

18. _____   39. _____

19. _____   40. _____

20. _____   41. _____

21. _____   42. _____

Activity Three: The Cabinet

DIRECTIONS: Using an almanac, find the names of the current Cabinet officers. Match the names with the departments they head.

DEPARTMENT   **NAME OF SECRETARY**

STATE (foreign affairs)   _____

TREASURY (money)   _____

DEFENSE (armed forces)   _____

JUSTICE (Attorney General; legal issues)   _____

INTERIOR (U.S. lands)   _____

AGRICULTURE (farming)   _____

COMMERCE (business)   _____

LABOR (working conditions)   _____

HEALTH AND HUMAN SERVICES
    (health and welfare)   _____

HOUSING AND URBAN DEVELOPMENT
    (housing and cities)   _____

TRANSPORTATION (roads, etc.)   _____

ENERGY (research on energy)   _____

EDUCATION (nation's schools)   _____

VETERANS' AFFAIRS (war veterans)   _____

Activity Four: Justices, Senators, and Representatives

DIRECTIONS: Using an almanac, find the names of the following government officials.

THE SUPREME COURT JUSTICES

YEAR APPOINTED

1. _____ , Chief Justice   _____

2. _____ , Associate Justice   _____

3. _____ , Associate Justice   _____

4. _____ , Associate Justice   _____

5. _____ , Associate Justice   _____

6. _____ , Associate Justice   _____

7. _____ , Associate Justice   _____

8. _____ , Associate Justice   _____

9. _____ , Associate Justice   _____

YOUR SENATORS:

   1. _____

   2. _____

YOUR REPRESENTATIVE:

   1. _____

OFFICERS OF THE HOUSE OF REPRESENTATIVES:

   1. _____ , Speaker of the House

OFFICERS OF THE SENATE:

   1. _____ , Vice President of the U.S.

   2. _____ , President Pro Tempore

Name _____

Date _____

EXECUTIVE BRANCH OF THE UNITED STATES GOVERNMENT

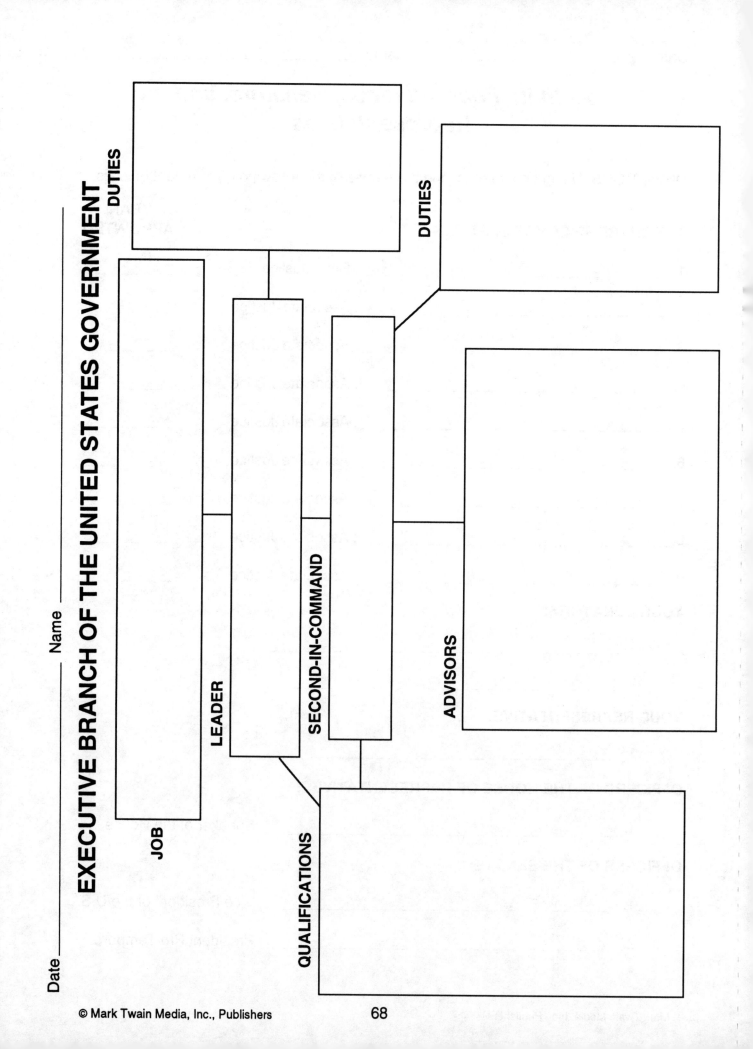

JOB

LEADER

SECOND-IN-COMMAND

QUALIFICATIONS

DUTIES

DUTIES

ADVISORS

LEGISLATIVE BRANCH OF THE UNITED STATES GOVERNMENT

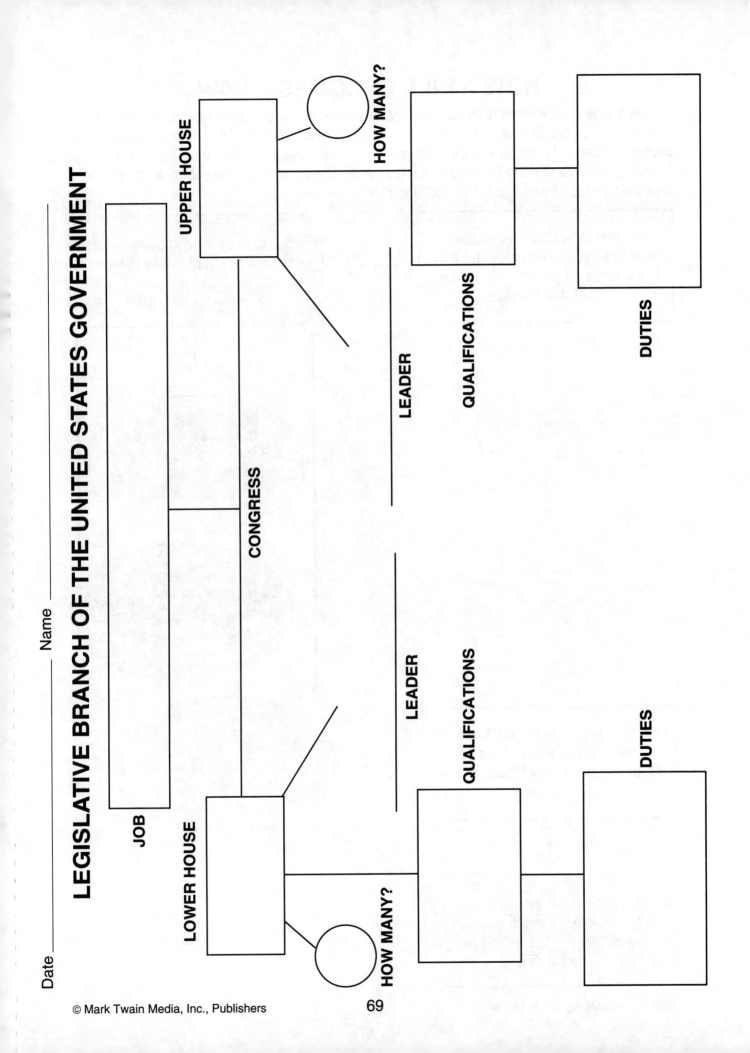

JOB

CONGRESS

UPPER HOUSE

HOW MANY?

LEADER

QUALIFICATIONS

DUTIES

LOWER HOUSE

HOW MANY?

LEADER

QUALIFICATIONS

DUTIES

69

HOW A BILL BECOMES A LAW

This is the path a bill takes to become a law. In this example, the bill originates in the Senate. Bills may also be introduced in the House of Representatives. Study each step in the process. If the bill is approved by each group the first time it is presented, how many steps does it go through? If the President vetoes the bill but Congress votes to override the veto, how many steps must the bill go through?

Senate Bill-200 is introduced, and the Senate votes on the bill. If approved, it goes to the House. If not, the bill dies.

If SB-200 is approved by the House, the bill is then sent to the President. If not, the bill goes back to the Senate for changes.

If the President signs SB-200 or doesn't sign it within ten working days, it becomes a law.

If the President doesn't sign SB-200 within ten days after Congress adjourns, the bill dies (pocket veto).

If the President vetoes SB-200, it goes back to the Senate.

If the Senate votes by a 2/3 majority to override the President's veto, the bill is sent to the House. If not, the bill dies.

If the House votes by a 2/3 majority to override the President's veto, the bill becomes a law. If not, the bill dies.

70

HOW A BILL BECOMES A LAW

Using what you have learned about the legislative process, trace House Bill-100 as it becomes a law. In each box describe what happens to the bill at that stage of the process. You may want to use the example from the previous page to help you. Actions by the House of Representatives are in rounded boxes, Senate actions are in square boxes, and Presidential actions are in ovals.

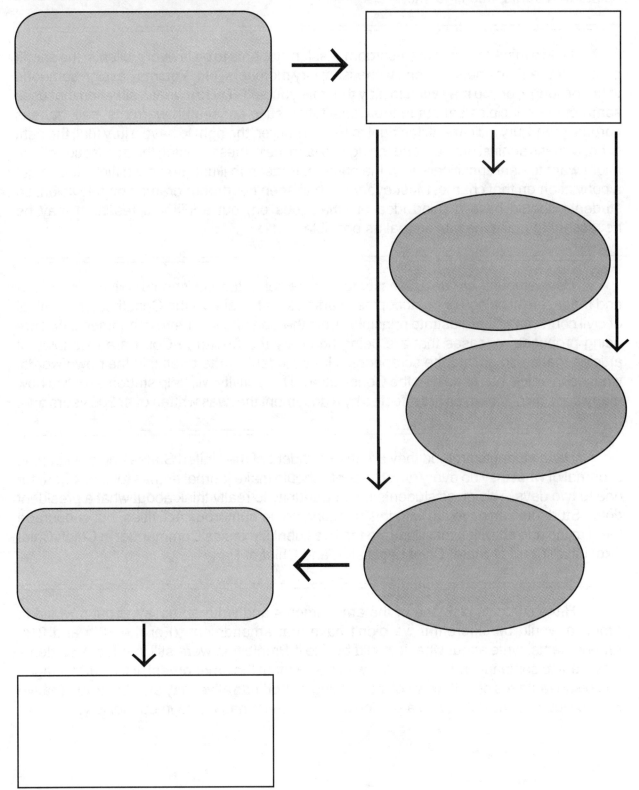

71

MORE CONSTITUTIONAL ACTIVITIES

Have each class member make up five questions about the Constitution. Then mix everyone's questions together, and divide the class into teams for a "Quiz Bowl" competition. Give points for correct answers, and when the game is over, reward the team with the most points with treats, free time, etc.

Hold a mock trial in your classroom. Assign students to be lawyers, clients, the sheriff or other law enforcement officers, witnesses, jury members, etc. You may assign someone to be the judge, or you may want to play that role yourself. Try to invent a situation that uses some of the principles set out in the Constitution such as: search warrants, bail, habeas corpus, grand jury indictment, the right to have a lawyer, the right to have a jury trial, the right to not witness against oneself, and the right to face the witness making the accusations. You might want to deal specifically with the crime of treason to illustrate how difficult it is to get a conviction on that charge. Most everyone has seen courtroom dramas on television, so students should have a good idea of what goes on, but additional research may be necessary to make the trial as real as possible.

Have students create a Constitution scrapbook. Students should collect newspaper and magazine clippings or photocopies of articles that deal with the Constitution. Criminal or civil court cases that illustrate principles from the Constitution, new amendments that are being proposed, or cases that are being heard by the Supreme Court are examples of articles that could go into the scrapbook. Have students write briefly, in their own words, what each article has to do with the Constitution. This activity will help students realize how many aspects of their lives are affected by a document that was written over 200 years ago!

Have students pretend they are the President of the United States and are keeping a journal of what they do every day. Students should make journal entries for every hour for one to two days. This gives students the opportunity to really think about what a president does. Students can have fun with this by listing some humorous activities, but encourage them to include activities that illustrate the President's roles as Commander in Chief, Chief Executive, Chief of State, Chief Legislator, and Chief of Party.

Have students pick one of the amendments and write an essay about how life in America would be different if we didn't have that amendment. (For the 18th and 21st Amendments, write about what it would be like if Prohibition were still in effect.) Students may want to compare and contrast life with and without the amendment, listing advantages and disadvantages of both ways of life. Writing a short narrative may also be an alternative way to illustrate the difference a particular amendment has made in our society.

Date _____   Name _____

UNITED STATES CONSTITUTION TEST

DIRECTIONS: Circle the correct answer to each question.

1. The Preamble
   a. states the purpose of the Declaration of Independence
   b. states the purpose of the Constitution
   c. concludes the Constitution
   d. influenced the War for Independence

2. The man who wrote the Declaration of Independence was
   a. James Madison   c. Thomas Jefferson
   b. James Monroe   d. Thomas Paine

3. The war in which the colonies won their independence from England was the
   a. French and Indian War   c. Civil War
   b. Revolutionary War   d. Crimean War

4. Before the adoption of the Constitution, the newly independent states were joined by the
   a. Articles of Confederation   c. Mayflower Compact
   b. Magna Carta   d. Bill of Rights

5. The Constitutional Convention met in the city of
   a. Philadelphia   c. Boston
   b. New York   d. Trenton

6. The Preamble begins with
   a. When in the course of human events . . .
   b. We the citizens need to form . . .
   c. As people of the United States . . .
   d. We the people of the United States . . .

7. Which of the following is not included in the Preamble?
   a. to form a more perfect union
   b. to promote the pursuit of happiness
   c. to provide for the common defense
   d. to establish justice

8. The plan of government proposed during the Constitutional Convention which called for a bicameral Congress based on population was the
   a. Florida Plan   c. New Jersey Plan
   b. Great Compromise   d. Virginia Plan

9. The Constitution needed the approval of how many states?
   a. seven
   b. nine
   c. thirteen
   d. five

10. The United States Constitution went into effect
   a. June 21, 1787
   b. June 21, 1788
   c. June 21, 1791
   d. June 21, 1970

11. Power in the United States government is divided among
   a. two branches
   b. seven branches
   c. twenty-five branches
   d. three branches

12. Congress is divided into
   a. two branches
   b. three branches
   c. two houses
   d. three houses

13. The number of Articles in the U.S. Constitution is
   a. three
   b. two
   c. seven
   d. nine

14. The number of amendments that have been added to the Constitution is
   a. twenty-five
   b. twenty-seven
   c. ten
   d. sixteen

15. The number of representatives each state has in the House depends on
   a. how big the state is
   b. when the state was admitted
   c. the population of the state
   d. how rich the state is

16. U.S. Senators are elected for
   a. four years
   b. two years
   c. life
   d. six years

17. Members of the House of Representatives are elected for
   a. two years
   b. six years
   c. four years
   d. life

18. The total number of members in the House of Representatives is
   a. 435
   b. 453
   c. 100
   d. 50

19. The total number of U.S. senators is
   a. 435
   b. 354
   c. 100
   d. 50

20. All revenue (money) bills originate in the
   a. Senate
   b. House
   c. Executive Branch
   d. Judicial Branch

21. Impeachment charges are started by the
    a. President
    b. House of Representatives
    c. Supreme Court
    d. Senate

22. The power to declare war belongs to the
    a. President
    b. Chief Justice
    c. Congress
    d. Secretary of State

23. The presiding officer of the Senate is
    a. the Chief Justice
    b. the President
    c. the Speaker
    d. the Vice President

24. The executive branch
    a. makes laws
    b. explains laws
    c. carries out laws
    d. declares laws unconstitutional

25. The electoral college was established by the Constitutional Convention because
    a. the founding fathers wanted to keep the common people from making a mistake
    b. they wanted a longer election period
    c. they wanted to confuse the American people
    d. none of the above

26. The judicial branch
    a. makes laws
    b. judges laws
    c. enforces laws
    d. vetoes laws

27. The number of justices on the Supreme Court is
    a. seven
    b. nine
    c. eleven
    d. fifteen

28. The current Chief Justice of the Supreme Court is
    a. Byron White
    b. Anthony Scalia
    c. Clarence Thomas
    d. William Renquist

29. The supreme law of the land is
    a. a state constitution
    b. a law passed by Congress
    c. a U.S. treaty
    d. the U.S. Constitution

30. The President of the U.S. does not have the power to
    a. declare war
    b. negotiate treaties
    c. appoint judges
    d. veto bills

31. The person who takes the President's place if he or she is unable to serve a full term is the
    a. President pro tempore
    b. Speaker of the House
    c. Chief Justice
    d. Vice President

32. The person who usually administers the oath of office to the President on Inauguration Day is the
    a. Speaker of the House   c. President pro tempore
    b. Chief Justice   d. Vice President

33. The term of justices of the Supreme Court is
    a. eight years   c. life
    b. ten years   d. six years

34. The first woman to be appointed a Supreme Court justice is
    a. Sandra Day O'Connor   c. Brenda Edgar
    b. Anita Hill   d. Elizabeth Dole

35. All appointments to the Supreme Court must be approved by
    a. the President Pro Tempore   c. the House
    b. the Speaker   d. the Senate

36. Impeachments are tried by the
    a. House   c. Supreme Court
    b. Senate   d. President

37. It punishes for something that was not illegal when it was done.
    a. bill of attainder   c. original jurisdiction
    b. writ of habeas corpus   d. ex post facto law

38. Type of law that punishes without a trial.
    a. appellate jurisdiction   c. ex post facto law
    b. writ of habeas corpus   d. bill of attainder

39. A person has the right to appear in person, in court.
    a. ex post facto law   c. bill of attainder
    b. writ of habeas corpus   d. judicial review

40. A formal request to the Supreme Court to hear a case is known as a
    a. writ of habeas corpus   c. bill of attainder
    b. writ of certiorari   d. ex post facto law

41. Bicameral means having _____ houses.
    a. one   c. three
    b. two   d. four

42. The executive branch checks (or controls) the legislative branch by
    a. vetoing laws
    b. passing laws over veto
    c. declaring laws unconstitutional
    d. controlling salaries

43. The legislative branch checks the executive branch by
    a. using the veto
    b. reducing the executive's salary
    c. declaring laws unconstitutional
    d. passing laws over a veto with a 2/3 vote

44. The legislative branch
    a. makes laws
    b. explains laws
    c. enforces laws
    d. vetoes laws

45. The section in the Constitution that gives Congress the power to pass laws "necessary and proper" to fulfill its other duties is the
    a. Preamble
    b. Elastic Clause
    c. Bill of Rights
    d. Judicial Review

46. Qualifications of a Supreme Court justice are
    a. the same as for the President
    b. the same as for a senator
    c. the same as for a member of the House of Representatives
    d. not stated in the Constitution

47. The first ten amendments to the Constitution are called
    a. the Bill of Rights
    b. the Civil Amendments
    c. the Preamble
    d. a bill of attainder

48. The number of members in the House of Representatives is based on _____, while the Senate is based on _____.
    a. population/equality
    b. population/population
    c. equality/population
    d. equality/equality

49. When the Supreme Court hears a case for the first time it is called
    a. appellate jurisdiction
    b. judicial review
    c. original jurisdiction
    d. due process of law

50. When the Supreme Court hears a case that has already been heard in a lower court it is called
    a. appellate jurisdiction
    b. double jeopardy
    c. original jurisdiction
    d. judicial review

51. Treason is
    a. talking against the U.S.
    b. not mentioned in the Constitution
    c. refusing to vote
    d. aiding the enemies of your country

52. State legislatures used to elect
    a. Senators   c. Representatives
    b. Presidents   d. Justices

53. Amendments can be proposed by
    a. 2/3 vote of each house of Congress
    b. 2/3 vote of the state senators
    c. conventions of 1/2 of the states
    d. legislatures of 3/4 of the states

54. Amendments can be ratified by
    a. 2/3 vote of each house of Congress
    b. legislatures of 2/3 of the states
    c. legislatures of 3/4 of the states
    d. conventions in 2/3 of the states

55. Which of the following is not a Cabinet department?
    a. State   c. Education
    b. Media   d. Treasury

56. Which of the following is an example of a government corporation?
    a. U.S. Postal Service   c. Labor Department
    b. Federal Communications Commission   d. NASA

57. Article V is important because it tells
    a. about the relationship between the states
    b. how the Constitution can be amended
    c. how the Constitution must be ratified
    d. about guarantees given to the states

58. The Preamble to the Constitution
    a. was added to the Constitution in 1791
    b. tells why the colonies declared their independence
    c. lists the grievances against the English government
    d. tells why the Constitution was written

59. Qualifications for the President are found in
    a. Article I (1)   c. Amendment XII (12)
    b. Article II (2)   d. Amendment XXII (22)

60. The name of the power (or responsibility) of the President that is associated with the military is
    a. Chief Executive   c. Chief of Party
    b. Commander in Chief   d. Chief Legislator

61. Treaties negotiated by the President must be approved by the
    a. Chief Justice
    b. Cabinet
    c. Senate
    d. Secretary of State

62. Has the power to admit new states
    a. President
    b. Supreme Court
    c. Congress
    d. President pro tempore

63. Tells how laws are made
    a. Article I (1)
    b. Article II (2)
    c. Article III (3)
    d. Article V (5)

64. Presides over the impeachment trial of a President
    a. Vice President
    b. Chief Justice
    c. Speaker of the House
    d. Attorney General

65. Who appoints justices to the Supreme Court?
    a. the President
    b. the Senate
    c. the Chief Justice
    d. the Vice President

66. Article which established the Supreme Court
    a. Article IV (4)
    b. Article II (2)
    c. Article III (3)
    d. Article I (1)

67. Powers that both the Federal and state governments have (such as taxation or road building) are known as
    a. delegated powers
    b. reserved powers
    c. inherent powers
    d. concurrent powers

68. Which branch of government is responsible for maintaining the army?
    a. Executive branch
    b. Legislative branch
    c. Judicial branch
    d. Both b and c

69. A person actually becomes President
    a. when he or she takes the oath of office
    b. on election day
    c. when he or she is nominated
    d. when the electoral college meets

70. A person appointed by the President to fill the vacant office of Vice President must be confirmed by
    a. a majority vote of the Senate
    b. a majority vote of the Supreme Court
    c. a majority vote of the House of Representatives
    d. a majority vote of both houses of Congress

71. The Constitution forbids the states to
    a. tax
    b. make laws
    c. coin money
    d. keep a militia

72. Powers of Congress are listed in
    a. Article I (1)
    b. Article II (2)
    c. Article III (3)
    d. Article IV (4)

73. A naturalized citizen cannot become
    a. a senator
    b. President
    c. a representative
    d. a justice

74. Presidents must be at least
    a. 25 years old
    b. 30 years old
    c. 35 years old
    d. 40 years old

75. Prohibits changes in salaries of U.S. senators and representatives from taking effect until after the next election.
    a. Amendment XII (12)
    b. Amendment XXVII (27)
    c. Amendment XVII (17)
    d. Amendment XXVI (26)

76. Slavery was abolished by
    a. Amendment III (3)
    b. Amendment XIII (13)
    c. Amendment IV (4)
    d. Amendment XIV (14)

77. Permits Congress to tax individual incomes
    a. Amendment VI (6)
    b. Amendment XXVI (26)
    c. Amendment XVI (16)
    d. Amendment XVII (17)

78. Gives residents of Washington, D.C., the right to vote
    a. Amendment XXII (22)
    b. Amendment XXIII (23)
    c. Amendment XXIV (24)
    d. Amendment XXV (25)

79. Forbids the manufacture and sale of alcoholic beverages
    a. Amendment XV (15)
    b. Amendment XVI (16)
    c. Amendment XVII (17)
    d. Amendment XVIII (18)

80. Moved Presidential inauguration day from March 4 to January 20
    a. Amendment XX (20)
    b. Amendment XXI (21)
    c. Amendment XXII (22)
    d. Amendment XXIII (23)

81. Limited President to two terms
    a. Amendment XII (12)
    b. Amendment VIII (8)
    c. Amendment III (3)
    d. Amendment XXII (22)

82. Powers not specifically given to the Federal government are reserved to the states or to the people
   a. Amendment VII (7)
   b. Amendment XVI (16)
   c. Amendment X (10)
   d. Amendment XXVI (26)

83. Guarantees that a person cannot be tried twice for the same crime
   a. Amendment XIV (14)
   b. Amendment XVI (16)
   c. Amendment V (5)
   d. Amendment I (1)

84. Denies state governments the power to keep citizens from voting by charging a poll tax
   a. Amendment XXIV (24)
   b. Amendment XIV (14)
   c. Amendment II (2)
   d. Amendment XXIII (23)

85. Forbids a state to stop a person from voting because of race or color
   a. Amendment I (1)
   b. Amendment II (2)
   c. Amendment XXVI (26)
   d. Amendment XV (15)

86. Right to bear arms
   a. Amendment IX (9)
   b. Amendment II (2)
   c. Amendment XI (11)
   d. Amendment XIV (15)

87. Prohibits quartering of troops in time of peace
   a. Amendment I (1)
   b. Amendment II (2)
   c. Amendment III (3)
   d. Amendment IV (4)

88. Safeguards against excessive bail, fines, and cruel and unusual punishments
   a. Amendment VII (7)
   b. Amendment VIII (8)
   c. Amendment IX (9)
   d. Amendment X (10)

89. Guarantees rights not listed to the people and that the government shouldn't tamper with them
   a. Amendment XIX (19)
   b. Amendment XVIII (18)
   c. Amendment IX (9)
   d. Amendment VIII (8)

90. Gives women the right to vote
   a. Amendment XIX (19)
   b. Amendment XVII (17)
   c. Amendment XVI (16)
   d. Amendment VI (6)

91. Tells what to do in case of Presidential disability
   a. Amendment XXIII (23)
   b. Amendment XXV (25)
   c. Amendment XXI (21)
   d. Amendment XXVI (26)

92. Lowers the voting age to 18
   a. Amendment XXVI (26)
   b. Amendment XXIV (24)
   c. Amendment XVI (16)
   d. Amendment XIV (14)

93. Provides for the election of President and Vice President on separate ballots
    a. Amendment XX (20)
    b. Amendment XXII (22)
    c. Amendment XII (12)
    d. Amendment II (2)

94. Gives the people the right to elect their senators directly
    a. Amendment VII (7)
    b. Amendment VI (6)
    c. Amendment XVII (17)
    d. Amendment XVI (16)

95. Protects against unreasonable search and arrest
    a. Amendment I (1)
    b. Amendment II (2)
    c. Amendment XVII (17)
    d. Amendment IV (4)

96. Gives citizenship to former slaves
    a. Amendment XIII (13)
    b. Amendment XIV (14)
    c. Amendment XV (15)
    d. Amendment XVI (16)

97. Provides that a state cannot be sued in any court other than the courts of that state. In other words, you can't sue a state in a Federal court.
    a. Amendment IX (9)
    b. Amendment X (10)
    c. Amendment XI (11)
    d. Amendment XII (12)

98. Repealed the prohibition amendment
    a. Amendment XX (20)
    b. Amendment XXI (21)
    c. Amendment XVIII (18)
    d. Amendment XIX (19)

99. Protects freedom of religion, speech, press, assembly, and petition
    a. Amendment IV (4)
    b. Amendment III (3)
    c. Amendment II (2)
    d. Amendment I (1)

100. Guarantees the right to a speedy trial with, if needed, a court-appointed lawyer
    a. Amendment V (5)
    b. Amendment VI (6)
    c. Amendment VII (7)
    d. Amendment VIII (8)

ANSWERS TO CHALLEGES

The Articles of Confederation (pg. 2)
1. Confederation: an alliance, especially of states and nations.
Constitution: a document stating the system of basic laws and principles of a government, society, etc.
Commerce: the buying and selling of goods; trade.
2. The first form of government was The Articles of Confederation.
3. It began to govern the U.S. in March, 1781.
4. Nine states had to agree.
5. Congress could: declare war, make peace, make treaties, coin and borrow money, create post offices, admit new states, and create an army and navy.
6. Congress could not: tax, control or interfere with trade between the individual states.
7. They did not want to create a new king.
8. The Annapolis Convention met in September, 1786, to study the trade problem.
9. Another convention was scheduled for May, 1787, in Philadelphia, Pennsylvania, for "the sole and express purpose of revising the Articles of Confederation."

The Constitutional Convention (pg. 4)
1. Convention: an assembly.
Compromise: a settlement in which both sides give up something in order to reach an agreement.
Delegate: a person authorized to act for others; a representative.
2. The Constitutional Convention met in Philadelphia, Pennsylvania.
3. The Constitution was written during May, June, July, August, and September, 1787.
4. Rhode Island didn't send delegates.
5. George Washington was president of the convention.
6. The most serious task that faced delegates was how to achieve a balance between liberty and authority.
7. Answers could include two of the following: Benjamin Franklin, Alexander Hamilton, James Madison, and George Washington.
8. John Adams and Thomas Jefferson were absent.
9. Benjamin Franklin was the oldest delegate at 81.
10. Jonathan Dayton was the youngest delegate at 26.

Compromise (pg. 6)
1. Bicameral: having two legislative chambers.
Unicameral: having a single legislative chamber.
2. The Great Compromise resolved the question of how to set up the lawmaking body of our government. It dealt with how states should be represented in the legislature and who should have control—large or small states.
3. The Virginia Plan was supported by large states because the number of Congressmen would be determined by population; therefore, the larger states would control Congress.
4. The New Jersey Plan was supported by small states because each state would have the same number of representatives; therefore, small states would be equal with large states.
5. A. Virginia Plan
1. Two houses 2. Determined by population
B. New Jersey Plan
1. One house 2. Determined by equality
6. The Great Compromise called for a bicameral Congress. The first house was to be called the House of Representatives, with representatives elected by the people for two-year terms. The number of representatives each state could elect would depend on the population of the state. The second house was to be called the Senate, with senators elected by their state legislatures for six-year terms. Each state would have two senators.
7. A. Population.
B. Equality.

Separation of Powers (pg. 8)

1. Separation of Powers: power in the Federal government is divided between the executive, legislative, and judicial branches. Each branch has different responsibilities.

Checks and Balances: each branch of the Federal government looks out for and checks the power of the other two branches so that each branch is balanced by the other two.

Legislative: the branch of government that makes the laws to govern our country; the House of Representatives and the Senate.

Executive: the branch of government that carries out the laws passed by the legislative branch; headed by the President.

Judicial: the branch of government that interprets or defines laws; headed by the Supreme Court.

2. The legislative branch has the power to make laws. The executive branch has the power to carry out the laws. The judicial branch has the power to interpret or define the laws.

3. The powers are separated so that no one branch gets too powerful, and each branch is balanced by the other two.

4. The legislative branch makes the laws to govern our country.

5. The executive branch carries out the laws passed by the legislature.

6. The judicial branch interprets or defines the laws.

7. The legislative branch checks the executive and judicial branches.

8. The executive branch checks the legislative and judicial branches.

9. The judicial branch checks the legislative and executive branches.

Organization of the Constitution (pg. 11)

1. Ratify: to formally approve.
Amend: to change or revise.
Article: one of the sections of a document.

2. The Constitution was approved by the Convention on September 17, 1787.

3. The Constitution was approved by the states on June 21, 1788.

4. The sun may represent the rising of the new nation of the United States of America.

5. The preamble is the introduction to the Constitution.

6. There are seven Articles in the Constitution.

7. Article I is about the legislative branch. Article II is about the executive branch. Article III is about the judicial branch.

8. There have been 27 amendments to the Constitution.

9. The italics indicate parts no longer in effect due to the passage of time or changes made by the amendments.

The Preamble (pg. 13)

1. The Constitution was written by the power of the people.

2. a. to form a more perfect union
b. establish justice
c. ensure domestic tranquility
d. provide for the common defense
e. promote the general welfare
f. secure the blessings of liberty to ourselves and our posterity

3. Answers will vary.

The Legislative Branch: Introduction (pg. 15)

1. Majority: one over half; the larger group of politicians.
Minority: one less than half; the smaller group of politicians.
Privilege: a special right, favor, etc. granted to some person or group.
Expel: to remove.

2. The major duty of the legislative branch is to make our country's laws.

3. The legislative body of our Federal government is called Congress.

4. The Congress meets in the Capitol Building in Washington, D.C.

5. Congress is made up of the House of Representatives and the Senate.

6. Congress begins its meetings on the third day of January every odd-numbered year.

7. The record of the meetings of Congress is called the *Congressional Record.*

8. Two privileges of Congress members are: they cannot be arrested when going to or from Congress or while attending a session of Congress, and they cannot be sued or punished for anything they might say in Congress.

The House of Representatives (pg. 17)

1. Census: a count of the people.
Impeach: to accuse an official of wrongdoing or misuse of power.

2. There are 435 representatives in the House.

3. Answers will vary.

4. At this printing, last census: 1990, next census: 2000.

5. The population of the U.S. at the last census (1990) was 248,709,873.

6. a. must be at least 25 years old
b. must be a citizen of the U.S. for at least seven years
c. must live in the state from which he or she is elected

7. The presiding officer is the Speaker of the House.

8. The House begins the impeachment process by accusing the official of some wrongdoing or misuse of power.

The Senate (pg. 19)

1. The two houses of Congress are the House of Representatives and the Senate.

2. Each state has two Senators.

3. There are 100 Senators.

4. The term of office for a senator is six years.

5. The term of office for a representative is two years.

6. a. must be at least 30 years old
b. must be a citizen of the U.S. for at least nine years
c. must live in the state he or she represents

7. The Vice President of the United States is the presiding officer of the Senate. If the Vice President is absent, the senators choose an alternate presiding officer, called the president pro tempore.

8. The Senate acts as the jury and tries impeachment cases.

Rules, Rights, and Privileges of Congress (pg. 21)

1. Quorum: one person over half the number of members; the minimum number who must be present in order to conduct business.
Expel: to remove.
Adjourn: to stop meeting.

2. There would have to be 218 representatives present to be a quorum.

3. Two thirds of the Senate must agree to expel a member. (66)

4. The notes of the meetings of Congress are published in the *Congressional Record.*

5. Representatives and senators are paid by the U.S. government.

6. Only the House may begin bills to raise money.

How Bills Become Laws (pg. 23)

1. Veto: to reject a bill and prevent it from becoming a law.
Override: to declare null and void.

2. A bill may be introduced in either the House or the Senate.

3. Money bills must be introduced in the House of Representatives.

4. It must go to the Senate.

5. It is given to the President for his approval.

6. The bill goes back to the house where it started, and both houses must vote to pass the bill over the President's veto.

7. Two thirds of both houses must agree to override the President's veto.

8. If the veto is not overridden, the bill is dead.

Powers of Congress (pg. 25)

1. Accept any four powers listed in Article I, Section 8.

2. The "elastic clause" is Article I, Section 8, Clause 18, which gives Congress the power "to make all laws which shall be necessary and proper" to carry out its responsibilities.

3. Enumerated powers are those specifically given to the Congress by the Constitution. The power to declare war is an example.

4. Implied powers are general powers given to Congress. They are stated but not enough information is given in the Constitution about details. For example: the power to establish post offices and post roads.

5. Inherent powers are unlisted powers that a government must have simply because it is a government and needs to run its affairs smoothly. The U.S. must deal with foreign countries diplomatically, but that power is not stated in the Constitution.

Limits on Congress and the States (pg. 27)

1. Habeas Corpus literally means " you shall have the body."

2. The Constitution prevents Congress from taking away the right to habeas corpus so that a person is allowed to be seen and heard in a courtroom by a judge.

3. A bill of attainder is a law passed by the government that convicts a person of a crime and punishes them without a trial.

4. An ex post facto law punishes people for a crime that was not a crime when they did it. For example: Mr. Z smoked on Monday. On Tuesday a law was passed prohibiting smoking. On Wednesday Mr. Z is arrested for smoking on Monday.

5. Accept any one of: cannot tax products from a state, cannot give preference to any state's seaport, government money can only be spent by passing a law, Congress cannot issue titles of nobility.

6. a. States cannot make treaties with other countries.

b. States cannot coin their own money.

7. Delegated powers are those given to the national government in Washington, D.C. Concurrent powers are those shared between the national and state governments. Reserved powers are those that only the states have.

The Executive Branch: Introduction (pg. 29)

1. Execute: to carry out.

Executive: the branch of government that carries out and enforces laws passed by the legislative branch.

2. The executive branch enforces, or makes sure people are obeying, the laws.

3. The title of chief executive of the U.S. is the President. As of this printing: Bill Clinton.

4. The second-in-command is the Vice President.

As of this printing: Albert Gore, Jr.

5. The job of the electoral college is to choose the President and Vice President.

6. Answers will vary. (Total number of representatives and senators from the state.)

7. The electoral college was established to keep the ill-informed common people from making a mistake and electing a disastrous leader.

8. The House of Representatives chooses the President in the event of a tie.

Qualifications for President (pg. 31)

1. a. must be a natural-born citizen of the United States

b. must be at least 35 years old

c. must have been a resident of the United States for at least 14 years

2. Succession to the presidency:

a. Vice President

b. Speaker of the House

c. President pro tempore of the Senate

d. Secretary of State

3. The current salary is $200,000 a year.

4. The President is elected on the first Tuesday after the first Monday in November. The President is inaugurated on January 20. Answers may vary.

5. The Chief Justice of the Supreme Court usually administers the oath of office to the President.

Powers and Duties of the President (pg. 32)

1. a. Commander in Chief
b. Chief Executive
c. Chief of State
d. Chief Legislator
e. Chief of Party
2. a. Commander in Chief of the United States Armed Forces.
b. All decisions regarding the Army, Navy, Air Force, and Marines are the responsibility of the President. He can also call the National Guard (state militias) from the individual states into the service of the United States.
3. a. Chief Executive.
b. The President as Chief Executive makes sure all of his cabinet, staff, and other employees are doing their jobs correctly.
4. a. Chief of State.
b. The President represents the U.S. when he or she travels to other countries, greets and hosts other foreign dignitaries when they visit the U.S., and may also make treaties with other countries, subject to approval of two thirds of the Senate.
5. a. Chief Legislator.
b. The President has the power to approve or disapprove (veto) of laws Congress makes. He can also suggest that certain laws be made by working with his supporters in the House or Senate.
6. a. Chief of Party.
b. He is the head of his political party and makes decisions regarding the make-up of his individual political party.

Impeachment (pg. 35)

1. Impeach: to accuse some official of wrongdoing or misuse of power.
Misdemeanor: any offense of lesser gravity than a felony.
Bribery: the act of offering someone an inducement, especially to do something wrong or illegal.
Treason: betrayal of one's country to an enemy. Defined in the Constitution as levying war against the United States, or in adhering to the enemies of the United States giving them aid and comfort.
2. The House of Representatives begins the impeachment process.
3. The Senate acts as the jury and tries the case.
4. The Chief Justice of the Supreme Court acts as the judge when the President is being tried.
5. Two thirds of the Senate must agree in order for the official to be removed from office.
6. Andrew Johnson went through the entire impeachment process in 1867-68.
7. Richard Nixon resigned before the House could vote on impeachment charges August 9, 1974.
8. No one has been removed from office by being found guilty.

Organization of the Executive Branch and the Cabinet (pg. 37)

1. a. the Cabinet departments
b. independent agencies
c. government corporations
d. regulatory agencies
2. There are fourteen Cabinet departments.
3. The title of the head of the Department of Defense is the Secretary of Defense.
4. Accept any three Cabinet departments except Defense.
5. George Washington created the Cabinet in 1789.
6. The National Aeronautics and Space Administration (NASA) is an independent agency.
7. The United States Postal Service or the Federal Deposit Insurance Corporation (FDIC) are examples of government corporations.
8. The Federal Communications Commission or the Federal Aviation Administration are regulatory commissions.

Organization of the Judicial Branch (pg. 39)

1. Judicial: branch of government having to do with the court system.
Appeal: a request for a case to be transferred

to a higher court for a rehearing.

2. The judicial branch interprets or explains the laws.

The legislative branch makes the laws.

The executive branch carries out the laws.

3. The highest court in the United States is the Supreme Court.

4. Men and women who serve on the Supreme Court are called justices.

5. Nine justices serve on the Supreme Court. They serve for life.

6. The President appoints justices and they must be approved by the Senate.

7. 91 district courts and 12 appeals courts.

8. Accept two of the following: Court of Military Appeals, United States Tax Court, and the United States Claims Courts.

Cases for the Supreme Court (pg. 41)

1. Jurisdiction: the power to hear cases.

2. a. the Constitution

b. federal laws

c. treaties

d. laws governing ships

e. ambassadors or public ministers

f. the U.S. government itself

g. two or more state governments

h. citizens of different states

i. a state or its citizens versus a foreign country or foreign citizen

3. Original jurisdiction is the power to hear a case first.

4. Appellate jurisdiction is having the power to hear a case only after it has gone through the lower court system.

5. A writ of certiorari is a formal request for the Supreme Court to hear a case.

Judicial Review and Treason (pg. 43)

1. Unconstitutional: going against or contrary to the Constitution of the United States.

Treason: carrying on war against the United States and giving help to the nation's enemies.

2. The process of checking the laws is called judicial review.

3. It means the law is void because the Constitution is the supreme law of the land.

4. Answers may vary.

5. In order to be convicted of treason, two witnesses must testify to the same story, and/or the accused must make a confession in the courtroom.

6. The executive branch carries out the laws.

7. The judicial branch interprets, or defines, the laws.

8. The legislative branch makes the laws.

Article IV: The States (pg. 45)

1. Republican: a form of government in which the power rests with representatives elected by the people.

2. Article IV deals with the roles of the states in the new government.

3. Oregon must respect the laws of Idaho.

4. Congress was given the power to admit new states.

5. Yes, if the legislatures of all three states and Congress approve, they could join together to form a new state.

6. A republican form of government is elected by the people.

7. Under the Articles of Confederation there was a mediocre friendship between states.

8. The Constitution set up a strong central government with the states respecting each other but being subject to the power of the Federal government.

Amending the Constitution (pg. 47)

1. Amend: to change or revise.

Ratify: to formally approve.

2. Article V provides a way for the Constitution to be amended.

3. a. Two thirds of both houses of Congress must agree to propose the amendment.

b. Two thirds of state legislatures may call constitutional conventions to propose an amendment.

4. a. Three fourths of the state legislatures must ratify the amendment.

b. Three fourths of the state's constitutional conventions must ratify the amendment.

5. Two thirds must propose an amendment, and three fourths must ratify it.

Articles VI and VII (pg. 49)

1. The framers wanted to confirm the authority of the Constitution by making it the "supreme law of the land."
2. No, because the Constitution says only Congress can make treaties with foreign countries.
3. Nine states had to approve the Constitution.
4. The Constitution was signed September 17, 1787.
5. It was 12 years after the Declaration of Independence.
6. The United States was being governed by the Articles of Confederation.
7. Answers will vary. Accept any four valid names.

The Amendments: Introduction (pg. 51)

1. There are 27 Amendments.
2. The first ten amendments are called the Bill of Rights.
3. The first ten amendments were added in 1791.
4. The most recent amendment was added in 1992, and the 27th Amendment put limits on Congressional pay raises.
5. The 13th Amendment abolished slavery in 1865.
6. The 19th Amendment gave women the right to vote.
7. The 1st Amendment guarantees the freedom of religion.
8. Amendments have been made due to changes in American society, because people felt there were rights that should have been included in the Constitution, and to change sections of the Constitution.

The Bill of Rights, 1791: Amendments I-III (pg. 53)

1. Assembly: the right to gather together in a group.
Petition: the right to ask the government to change things.
Quartering: to furnish with lodgings.
2. The states insisted that a Bill of Rights be added to list the rights that should be protected for all Americans.

3. a. freedom of religion
b. freedom of speech
c. freedom of the press
d. freedom of assembly
e. right of petition
4. The Second Amendment gives Americans the right to bear arms (own weapons or guns).
5. The Third Amendment outlaws the quartering, or housing, of soldiers in private homes in peacetime.
6. Answers may vary, but the Supreme Court has said that the freedom of speech may be curbed when it poses a "clear and present danger" to others (*Schenk v. United States*).

The Bill of Rights, 1791: Amendments IV-VI (pg. 55)

1. A search warrant is a document issued by a judge to the sheriff for the purpose of getting evidence concerning a crime.
2. An arrest warrant is a document issued for the purpose of arresting someone suspected of a crime.
3. A grand jury is a group of people who decide if there is enough evidence to have a trial.
4. An indictment is a formal charge or accusation against a person.
5. Double jeopardy is being tried twice for the same crime.
6. The Fifth Amendment.
7. The Fourth Amendment.
8. The Fifth Amendment.
9. The Sixth Amendment.
10. The Fifth Amendment.

The Bill of Rights, 1791: Amendments VII-X (pg. 57)

1. A jury is a group of peers sworn to hear evidence in a law case and give a decision.
2. The Seventh Amendment guarantees the right to a trial by a jury in any case involving more than twenty dollars.
3. Excessive bail is having to pay an amount to be released from jail that is much more than the severity of the crime calls for.
4. Answers will vary.

5. The Eighth Amendment protects us from having to pay excessive bail and being punished in cruel and unusual ways.

6. The Ninth Amendment says rights not listed in the Constitution are given to the people.

7. The states have the power to set up schools.

8. There are ten amendments in the Bill of Rights.

1798-1870: Amendments XI-XV (pg. 59)

1. a. 1798
b. 1804
c. 1865
d. 1868
e. 1870

2. The Twelfth Amendment allowed voters to vote for the President and Vice President on separate ballots so that members of the same political party would not be running against each other for the presidency.

3. The Thirteenth Amendment was a result of the Civil War.

4. The Thirteenth Amendment abolished slavery.

5. All Americans, regardless of race, are guaranteed the rights listed in the Constitution.

6. Suffrage is the right to vote.

7. The Fifteenth Amendment gave black males the right to vote.

8. The Eleventh to Fifteenth Amendments were ratified between 1791 and 1870.

1900-1950: Amendments XVI-XXI (pg. 61)

1. Prohibition: the time period in which the production, sale, and use of alcoholic beverages was prohibited in the United States.

2. a. 1913
b. 1913
c. 1919
d. 1920
e. 1933
f. 1933

3. establish an income tax.

4. Senators were elected by the state legislatures before the Seventeenth Amendment. Now the people elect senators.

5. Many people saw the "evils of drinking" and felt the production, sale, and use of alcoholic beverages should be prohibited.

6. The Twenty-first Amendment repealed the Eighteenth Amendment.

7. The Nineteenth Amendment gave women the right to vote.

8. The Twentieth Amendment changed the date when elected officials took office, because there had been a long period of time between the election and when they took office.

1950-Present: Amendments XXII-XXVII (pg. 63)

1. a. 1950
b. 1961
c. 1964
d. 1967
e. 1971
f. 1992

2. A person can be elected to two terms as President.

3. The Twenty-third Amendment gave citizens of the District of Columbia the right to vote.

4. The Twenty-sixth Amendment gave 18-year-olds the right to vote.

5. The Twenty-fourth Amendment outlawed the poll tax.

6. The new President appoints a Vice President, and the new Vice President must be approved by a majority vote of both houses of Congress.

7. Twenty-fifth Amendment.

8. Changes in the salaries of senators and representatives will not take effect until after the next election.

9. 203 years.

ANSWERS TO ACTIVITY ONE
THE UNITED STATES IN RATIFICATION ORDER (PG. 64)

1. Delaware	December 7, 1787	26. Michigan	January 16, 1845
2. Pennsylvania	December 12, 1787	27. Florida	March 3, 1845
3. New Jersey	December 18, 1787	28. Texas	December 29, 1845
4. Georgia	January 2, 1788	29. Iowa	December 28, 1846
5. Connecticut	January 9, 1788	30. Wisconsin	May 29, 1848
6. Massachusetts	February 6, 1788	31. California	September 9, 1850
7. Maryland	April 28, 1788	32. Minnesota	May 11, 1858
8. South Carolina	May 23, 1788	33. Oregon	February 14, 1859
9. New Hampshire	June 21, 1788	34. Kansas	January 29, 1861
10. Virginia	June 25, 1788	35. West Virginia	June 19, 1863
11. New York	July 26, 1788	36. Nevada	October 31, 1864
12. North Carolina	November 21, 1789	37. Nebraska	March 1, 1867
13. Rhode Island	May 29, 1790	38. Colorado	August 1, 1876
14. Vermont	March 4, 1791	39. North Dakota	November 2, 1889
15. Kentucky	June 1, 1792	40. South Dakota	November 2, 1889
16. Tennessee	June 1, 1796	41. Montana	November 8, 1889
17. Ohio	March 1, 1803	42. Washington	November 11, 1889
18. Louisiana	April 30, 1812	43. Idaho	July 3, 1890
19. Indiana	December 11, 1816	44. Wyoming	July 10, 1890
20. Mississippi	December 10, 1817	45. Utah	January 4, 1896
21. Illinois	December 3, 1818	46. Oklahoma	November 16, 1907
22. Alabama	December 14, 1819	47. New Mexico	January 6, 1912
23. Maine	March 15, 1820	48. Arizona	February 14, 1912
24. Missouri	August 10, 1821	49. Alaska	January 3, 1959
25. Arkansas	June 15, 1836	50. Hawaii	August 21, 1959

ANSWERS TO ACTIVITY TWO
PRESIDENTS OF THE UNITED STATES (PG. 65)

1. George Washington
2. John Adams
3. Thomas Jefferson
4. James Madison
5. James Monroe
6. John Quincy Adams
7. Andrew Jackson
8. Martin Van Buren
9. William H. Harrison
10. John Tyler
11. James K. Polk
12. Zachary Taylor
13. Millard Fillmore
14. Franklin Pierce
15. James Buchanan
16. Abraham Lincoln
17. Andrew Johnson
18. Ulysses S. Grant
19. Rutherford B. Hayes
20. James A. Garfield
21. Chester A. Arthur
22. Grover Cleveland
23. Benjamin Harrison
24. Grover Cleveland
25. William McKinley
26. Theodore Roosevelt
27. William Howard Taft
28. Woodrow Wilson
29. Warren G. Harding
30. Calvin Coolidge
31. Herbert Hoover
32. Franklin D. Roosevelt
33. Harry S Truman
34. Dwight D. Eisenhower
35. John F. Kennedy
36. Lyndon B. Johnson
37. Richard M. Nixon
38. Gerald R. Ford
39. Jimmy Carter
40. Ronald Reagan
41. George Bush
42. Bill Clinton

ANSWERS TO UNITED STATES CONSTITUTION TEST (PG. 73)

1. B	34. A	67. D
2. C	35. D	68. B
3. B	36. B	69. A
4. A	37. D	70. D
5. A	38. D	71. C
6. D	39. B	72. A
7. B	40. B	73. B
8. D	41. B	74. C
9. B	42. A	75. B
10. B	43. D	76. B
11. D	44. A	77. C
12. C	45. B	78. B
13. C	46. D	79. D
14. B	47. A	80. A
15. C	48. A	81. D
16. D	49. C	82. C
17. A	50. A	83. C
18. A	51. D	84. A
19. C	52. A	85. D
20. B	53. A	86. B
21. B	54. C	87. C
22. C	55. B	88. B
23. D	56. A	89. C
24. C	57. B	90. A
25. A	58. D	91. B
26. B	59. B	92. A
27. B	60. B	93. C
28. D	61. C	94. C
29. D	62. C	95. D
30. A	63. A	96. B
31. D	64. B	97. C
32. B	65. A	98. B
33. C	66. C	99. D
		100. B

The Constitution of the United States

(Italicized words indicate portions of the Constitution that are no longer in effect.)

Preamble

We the people of the United States, in order to form a more perfect union, establish justice, insure domestic tranquility, provide for the common defense, promote the general welfare, and secure the blessings of liberty to ourselves and our posterity, do ordain and establish this Constitution for the United States of America.

ARTICLE I   *(Legislature)*

Section 1. All legislative powers herein granted shall be vested in a Congress of the United States, which shall consist of a Senate and a House of Representatives.

(House of Representatives)

Section 2. The House of Representatives shall be composed of members chosen every second year by the people of the several States, and the electors in each State shall have the qualifications requisite for electors of the most numerous branch of the State Legislature.

(Qualifications for Representatives)

No person shall be a Representative who shall not have attained to the age of twenty-five years, and been seven years a citizen of the United States, and who shall not, when elected, be an inhabitant of that State in which he shall be chosen.

(Method of Apportionment)

Representatives and direct taxes shall be apportioned among the several States which may be included within this Union, according to their respective numbers, *which shall be determined by adding to the whole number of free persons, including those bound to service for a term of years and excluding Indians not taxed, three-fifths of all other persons.* The actual enumeration shall be made within three years after the first meeting of the Congress of the United States, and within every subsequent term of ten years, in such manner as they shall by law direct. The number of Representatives shall not exceed one for every thirty thousand, but each state shall have at least one Representative; *and until such enumeration shall be made, the State of New Hampshire shall be entitled to choose three, Massachusetts eight, Rhode Island and Providence Plantations one, Connecticut five, New York six, New Jersey four, Pennsylvania eight, Delaware one, Maryland six, Virginia ten, North Carolina five, South Carolina five, and Georgia three.*

(Vacancies)

When vacancies happen in the representation from any State, the Executive authority thereof shall issue writs of election to fill such vacancies.

(Rules of the House, Impeachment)

The House of Representatives shall choose their Speaker and other officers; and shall have the sole power of impeachment.

(Senators)

Section 3. The Senate of the United States shall be composed of two Senators from each state, *chosen by the legislature thereof,* for six years; and each Senator shall have one vote.

Immediately after they shall be assembled in consequence of the first election, they shall be divided as equally as may be into three classes. The seats of the Senators of the first class shall be vacated at the expiration of the second year, of the second class at the expiration of the fourth year, and of the third class at the expiration of the sixth year, so that one-third may be chosen every second year; *and if vacancies happen by resignation or otherwise, during the recess of the legislature of any State, the Executive thereof may make temporary appointments until the next meeting of the legislature, which shall then fill such vacancies.*

(Qualifications of Senators)

No person shall be a Senator who shall not have attained to the age of thirty years, and been nine years a citizen of the United States, and who shall not, when elected, be an inhabitant of that State for which he shall be chosen.

(Vice President)

The Vice President of the United States shall be President of the Senate, but shall have no vote, unless they be equally divided.

The Senate shall choose their other officers, and also a President *pro tempore,* in the absence of the Vice President, or when he shall exercise the office of President of the United States.

(Impeachments)

The Senate shall have the sole power to try all impeachments. When sitting for that purpose, they shall be on oath or affirmation. When the President of the United States is tried, the Chief Justice shall preside; and no person shall be convicted without the concurrence of two-thirds of the members present.

Judgment in cases of impeachment shall not extend further than to removal from the office, and disqualification to hold and enjoy any office of honor, trust or profit under the United States: but the party convicted shall nevertheless be liable and subject to indictment, trial, judgment and punishment, according to law.

(Elections)

Section 4. The times, places and manner of holding elections for Senators and Representatives shall be prescribed in each

State by the legislature thereof; but the Congress may at any time by law make or alter such regulations, except as to the places of choosing Senators.

(Sessions)

The Congress shall assemble at least once in every year, and such meeting *shall be on the first Monday in December, unless they shall by law appoint a different day.*

(Proceedings of the House and the Senate)

Section 5. Each house shall be the judge of the elections, returns and qualifications of its own members, and a majority of each shall constitute a quorum to do business; but a smaller number may adjourn from day to day, and may be authorized to compel the attendance of absent members, in such manner, and under such penalties, as each house may provide.

Each house may determine the rules of its proceedings, punish its members for disorderly behavior, and with the concurrence of two-thirds, expel a member.

Each house shall keep a journal of its proceedings, and from time to time publish the same, excepting such parts as may in their judgment require secrecy; and the yeas and nays of the members of either house on any question shall, at the desire of one-fifth of those present, be entered on the journal.

Neither house, during the session of Congress, shall, without the consent of the other, adjourn for more than three days, nor to any other place than that in which the two houses shall be sitting.

(Members' Compensation and Privileges)

Section 6. The Senators and Representatives shall receive a compensation for their services, to be ascertained by law and paid out of the treasury of the United States. They shall in all cases except treason, felony and breach of the peace be privileged from arrest during their attendance at the session of their respective houses, and in going to and returning from the same; and for any speech or debate in either house, they shall not be questioned in any other place.

No Senator or Representative shall, during the time for which he was elected, be appointed to any civil office under the authority of the United States, which shall have been created, or the emoluments whereof shall have been increased, during such time; and no person holding any office under the United States shall be a member of either house during his continuance in office.

(Money Bills)

Section 7. All bills for raising revenue shall originate in the House of Representatives; but the Senate may propose or concur with amendments as on other bills.

(Presidential Veto and Congressional Power to Override)

Every bill which shall have passed the House of Representatives and the Senate, shall, before it becomes a law, be presented to the President of the United States; if he approve he shall sign it, but if not he shall return it with objections to that house in which it originated, who shall enter the objections at large on their journal, and proceed to reconsider it. If after such reconsideration two-thirds of that house shall agree to pass the bill, it shall be sent, together with the objections, to the other house, by which it shall likewise be reconsidered, and, if approved by two-thirds of that house, it shall become a law. But in all such cases the votes of both houses shall be determined by yeas and nays, and the names of the persons voting for and against the bill shall be entered on the journal of each house respectively. If any bill shall not be returned by the President within ten days (Sundays excepted) after it shall have been presented to him, the same

shall be a law, in like manner as if he had signed it, unless the Congress by their adjournment prevent its return, in which case it shall not be a law.

Every order, resolution, or vote to which the concurrence of the Senate and House of Representatives may be necessary (except on a question of adjournment) shall be presented to the President of the United States; and before the same shall take effect, shall be approved by him, or being disapproved by him, shall be repassed by two-thirds of the Senate and House of Representatives, according to the rules and limitations prescribed in the case of a bill.

(Congressional Powers)

Section 8. The Congress shall have power:

To lay and collect taxes, duties, imposts, and excises, to pay the debts and provide for the common defense and general welfare of the United States; but all duties, imposts and excises shall be uniform throughout the United States;

To borrow money on the credit of the United States;

To regulate commerce with foreign nations, and among the several States, and with the Indian tribes;

To establish an uniform rule of naturalization, and uniform laws on the subject of bankruptcies throughout the United States;

To coin money, regulate the value thereof, and of foreign coin, and fix the standard of weights and measures;

To provide for the punishment of counterfeiting the securities and current coin of the United States;

To establish post offices and post roads;

To promote the progress of science and useful arts by securing for limited times to authors and inventors the exclusive right to their respective writings and discoveries;

To constitute tribunals inferior to the Supreme Court;

To define and punish piracies and felonies committed on the high seas and offenses against the law of nations;

To declare war, grant letters of marque and reprisal, and make rules concerning captures on land and water;

To raise and support armies, but no appropriation of money to that use shall be for a longer term then two years;

To provide and maintain a navy;

To make rules for the government and regulation of the land and naval forces;

To provide for calling forth the militia to execute the laws of the Union, suppress insurrections, and repel invasions;

To provide for organizing, arming, and disciplining the militia, and for governing such part of them as may be employed in the service of the United States, reserving to the States respectively the appointment of the officers, and the authority of training the militia according to the discipline prescribed by Congress;

To exercise exclusive legislation in all cases whatsoever, over such district (not exceeding ten miles square) as may, by cession of particular States, and the acceptance of Congress, become the seat of government of the United States, and to exercise like authority over all places purchased by the consent of the legislature of the State, in which the same shall be, for erection of forts, magazines, arsenals, dockyards, and other needful buildings;—and

To make all laws which shall be necessary and proper for carrying into execution the foregoing powers, and all other powers vested by this Constitution in the government of the United States, or in any department or officer thereof.

(Limits on Congressional Power)
Section 9. *The migration or importation of such persons as any of the States now existing shall think proper to admit shall not be prohibited by the Congress prior to the year 1808; but a tax or duty may be imposed on such importation, not exceeding $10 for each person.*

The privilege of the writ of habeas corpus shall not be suspended, unless when in cases of rebellion or invasion the public safety may require it.

No bill of attainder or ex post facto law shall be passed.

No capitation or other direct tax shall be laid, unless in proportion to the census or enumeration herein before directed to be taken.

No tax or duty shall be laid on articles exported from any State.

No preference shall be given by any regulation of commerce or revenue to the ports of one State over those of another; nor shall vessels bound to, or from, one State be obliged to enter, clear, or pay duties in another.

No money shall be drawn from the treasury, but in consequence of appropriations made by law; and a regular statement and account of the receipts and expenditures of all public money shall be published from time to time.

No title of nobility shall be granted by the United States: and no person holding any office of profit or trust under them, shall, without the consent of the Congress, accept of any present, emolument, office, or title, of any kind whatever, from any king, prince, or foreign state.

(Limits on Powers of the States)
Section 10. No State shall enter into any treaty, alliance, or confederation; grant letters of marque and reprisal; coin money, emit bills of credit; make anything but gold and silver coin a tender in payment of debts; pass any bill of attainder, ex post facto law, or law impairing the obligation of contracts, or grant any title of nobility.

No States shall, without the consent of Congress, lay any imposts or duties on imports or exports, except what may be absolutely necessary for executing its inspection laws: and the net produce of all duties and imposts, laid by any State on imports or exports, shall be for the use of the treasury of the United States; and all such laws shall be subject to the revision and control of the Congress.

No State shall, without the consent of Congress, lay any duty of tonnage, keep troops or ships of war in time of peace, enter into any agreement or compact with another State, or with a foreign power, or engage in war, unless actually invaded, or in such imminent danger as will not admit of delay.

ARTICLE II   (Executive)

(President)

Section 1. The executive power shall be vested in a President of the United States of America. He shall hold his office during the term of four years, and, together with the Vice President, chosen for the same term, be elected as follows:

(Election of President)

Each State shall appoint, in such manner as the legislature thereof may direct, a number of electors, equal to the whole number of Senators and Representatives to which the State may be entitled in the Congress; but no Senator or Representative, or person holding an office of trust or profit under the United States, shall be appointed an elector.

(Electors)

The electors shall meet in their respective States, and vote by ballot for two persons, of whom one at least shall not be an inhabitant of the same State with themselves. And they shall make a list of all the persons voted for, and of the number of votes for each; which list they shall sign and certify, and transmit sealed to the seat of government of the United States, directed to the President of the Senate. The President of the Senate shall, in the presence of the Senate and House of Representatives, open all the certificates, and the votes shall then be counted. The person having the greatest number of votes shall be the President, if such number be a majority of the whole number of electors appointed; and if there be more than one who have such majority, and have an equal number of votes, then the House of Representatives shall immediately choose by ballot one of them for President; and if no person have a majority, then from the five highest on the list said house shall in like manner choose the President. But in choosing the President the votes shall be taken by States, the representation from each State having one vote; a quorum for this purpose shall consist of a member or members from two thirds of the States, and a majority of all the States shall be necessary to a choice. In every case, after the choice of the President, the person having the greatest number of votes of the electors shall be the Vice President. But if there should remain two or more who have equal votes, the Senate shall choose from them by ballot the Vice President.

The Congress may determine the time of choosing the electors and the day on which they shall give their votes; which day shall be the same throughout the United States.

(Qualifications of President)

No person except a natural-born citizen, or a citizen of the United States at the time of the adoption of the Constitution, shall be eligible to the office of President; neither shall any person be eligible to that office who shall not have attained to the age of thirty-five years, and been fourteen years a resident within the United States.

(Succession to the Presidency)

In case of the removal of the President from office or of his death, resignation, or inability to discharge the powers and duties of the said office, the same shall devolve on the Vice President, and the Congress may by law provide for the case of removal, death, resignation, or inability, both of the President and Vice President, declaring what officer shall then act as President, and such officer shall act accordingly, until the disability be removed, or a President shall be elected.

(Compensation)

The President shall, at stated times, receive for his services a compensation, which shall neither be increased nor diminished during the period for which he shall have been elected, and he shall not receive within that period any other emolument from the United States, or any of them.

(Oath of Office)

Before he enter on the execution of his office, he shall take the following oath or affirmation:—"I do solemnly swear (or affirm) that I will faithfully execute the office of the President of the United States, and will to the best of my ability preserve, protect and defend the Constitution of the United States."

(Powers of the President)

Section 2. The President shall be commander in chief of the army and navy of the United States, and of the militia of the several States, when called into the actual service of the United States; he may require the opinion, in writing, of the principal officer in each of the executive departments, upon any subject relating to the duties of their respective offices, and he shall have power to grant reprieves and pardons for offenses against the United States, except in cases of impeachment.

(Making of Treaties)

He shall have power, by and with the advice and consent of the Senate, to make treaties, provided two-thirds of the Senators present concur; and he shall nominate, and by and with the advice and consent of the Senate, shall appoint ambassadors, other public ministers and consuls, judges of the Supreme Court, and all other officers of the United States, whose appointments are not herein otherwise provided for, and which shall be established by law: but Congress may by law vest the appointment of such inferior officers, as they think proper, in the President alone, in the courts of law, or in the heads of departments.

(Vacancies)

The President shall have power to fill up all vacancies that may happen during the recess of the Senate, by granting commissions which shall expire at the end of their next session.

(Additional Duties and Powers)

Section 3. He shall from time to time give to the Congress information of the state of the Union, and recommend to their consideration such measures as he shall judge necessary and expedient; he may, on extraordinary occasions, convene both houses, or either of them, and in case of disagreement between them, with respect to the time of adjournment, he may adjourn them to such time as he shall think proper; he shall receive ambassadors and other public ministers; he shall take care that the laws be faithfully executed, and shall commission all the officers of the United States.

(Impeachment)

Section 4. The President, Vice President and all civil officers of the United States shall be removed from office on impeachment for, and on conviction of, treason, bribery, or other high crimes and misdemeanors.

ARTICLE III   (Judiciary)

(Courts, Judges, Compensation)

Section 1. The judicial power of the United States shall be vested in one Supreme

Court, and in such inferior courts as the Congress may from time to time ordain and establish. The judges, both of the Supreme and inferior courts, shall hold their offices during good behavior, and shall, at stated times, receive for their services a compensation which shall not be diminished during their continuance in office.

(Jurisdiction)

Section 2. The judicial power shall extend to all cases, in law and equity, arising under this Constitution, the laws of the United States, and treaties made, or which shall be made, under their authority—to all cases affecting ambassadors, other public ministers and consuls;—to all cases of admiralty and maritime jurisdiction;—to controversies to which the United States shall be a party;—to controversies between two or more States;— *between a State and citizens of another State;*—between citizens of different States;—between citizens of the same State claiming lands under grants of different States, and between a State, or the citizens thereof, and foreign states, citizens or subjects.

In all cases affecting ambassadors, other public ministers and consuls, and those in which a State shall be party, the Supreme Court shall have original jurisdiction. In all the other cases before mentioned, the Supreme Court shall have appellate jurisdiction, both as to law and fact, with such exceptions, and under such regulations, as the Congress shall make.

(Trial by Jury)

The trial of all crimes, except in cases of impeachment, shall be by jury; and such trial shall be held in the State where said crimes shall have been committed; but when not committed within any State, the trial shall be at such place or places as the Congress may by law have directed.

(Treason)

Section 3. Treason against the United States shall consist only in levying war against them, or in adhering to their enemies, giving them aid and comfort. No person shall be convicted of treason unless on the testimony of two witnesses to the same overt act, or on confession in open court.

The Congress shall have power to declare the punishment of treason, but no attainder of treason shall work corruption of blood, or forfeiture except during the life of the person attained.

ARTICLE IV   *(Federal System)*

Section 1. Full faith and credit shall be given in each State to the public acts, records, and judicial proceedings of every other State. And the Congress may by general laws prescribe the manner in which such acts, records, and proceedings shall be proved, and the effect thereof.

(Privileges and Immunities of Citizens)

Section 2. The citizens of each State shall be entitled to all privileges and immunities of citizens in the several States. A person charged in any State with treason, felony, or other crime, who shall flee from justice, and be found in another State, shall on demand of the executive authority of the State from which he fled, be delivered up, to be removed to the State having jurisdiction of the crime.

No person held to service or labor in one State, under the laws thereof, escaping into another, shall, in consequence of any law or regulation therein, be discharged from such service or labor, but shall be delivered up on claim of the party to whom such service or labor may be due.

(Admission and Formation of New States; Governing of Territories)

Section 3. New States may be admitted by the Congress into this Union; but no new State shall be formed or erected within the jurisdiction of any other State; nor any State be formed by the junction of two or more States, or parts of States, without the consent of the legislatures of the States concerned as well as of the Congress.

The Congress shall have power to dispose of and make all needful rules and regulations respecting the territory or other property belonging to the United States; and nothing in this Constitution shall be so construed as to prejudice any claims of the United States, or of any particular State.

(Federal Protection of the States)

Section 4. The United States shall guarantee to every State in this Union a republican form of government, and shall protect each of them against invasion; and on application of the legislature, or of the executive (when the legislature cannot be convened), against domestic violence.

ARTICLE V — *(Amendments)*

The Congress, whenever two-thirds of both houses shall deem it necessary, shall propose amendments to this Constitution, or, on the application of the legislatures of two-thirds of the several States, shall call a convention for proposing amendments, which, in either case, shall be valid to all intents and purposes, as part of this Constitution, when ratified by the legislatures of three-fourths of the several States, or by conventions in three-fourths thereof, as the one of the other mode of ratification may be proposed by the Congress; provided *that no amendments which may be made prior to the year one thousand eight hundred and eight shall in any manner affect the first and fourth clauses in the ninth section of the first article; and* that no State, without its consent, shall be deprived of its equal suffrage in the Senate.

ARTICLE VI — *(Constitution as Supreme Law)*

All debts contracted and engagements entered into, before the adoption of this Constitution, shall be as valid against the United States under this Constitution, as under the Confederation.

This Constitution, and the laws of the United States which shall be made in pursuance thereof; and all treaties made, or which shall be made, under the authority of the United States, shall be the supreme law of the land, and the judges in every State shall be bound thereby, anything in the Constitution or laws of any State to the contrary notwithstanding.

The Senators and Representatives before mentioned, and the members of the several State legislatures, and all executive and judicial officers, both of the United States and of the several States, shall be bound by oath or affirmation to support this Constitution; but no religious test shall ever be required as a qualification to any office or public trust under the United States.

ARTICLE VII — *(Ratification)*

The ratification of the conventions of nine States shall be sufficient for the establishment of the Constitution between the States so ratifying the same.

Done in Convention by the unanimous consent of the States present, the seventeenth day of September in the year of our Lord one thousand seven hundred and eighty-seven and of the Independence of the United States of America the twelfth. In witness whereof we have hereunto subscribed our names.

Go. Washington, *President and deputy from Virginia; Attest* William Jackson, *Secretary;*

Delaware: Geo. Read, Gunning Bedford, Jr., John Dickinson, Richard Bassett, Jaco. Broom; *Maryland:* James McHenry, Daniel of St. Thomas' Jenifer, Danl. Carroll; *Virginia:* John Blair, James Madison, Jr.; *North Carolina:* Wm. Blount, Richd. Dobbs Spaight, Hu Williamson; *South Carolina:* J. Rutledge, Charles Cotesworth Pinckney, Charles Pinckney, Pierce Butler; *Georgia:* William Few, Abr. Baldwin; *New Hampshire:* John Langdon, Nicholas Gilman; *Massachusetts:* Nathaniel Gorham, Rufus King; *Connecticut:* Wm. Saml. Johnson, Roger Sherman; *New York:* Alexander Hamilton; *New Jersey:* Wil. Livingston, David Brearley, Wm. Paterson, Jona. Dayton; *Pennsylvania:* B. Franklin, Thomas Mifflin, Robt. Morris, Geo. Clymer, Thos. FitzSimons, Jared Ingersoll, James Wilson, Gouv. Morris.

AMENDMENTS TO THE CONSTITUTION
(The first ten amendments are known as The Bill of Rights.)

AMENDMENT I [1791]   *(Freedoms)*

(Speech, Press, Assembly, and Petition)

Congress shall make no law respecting an establishment of religion, or prohibiting the free exercise thereof; or abridging the freedom of speech, or of the press; or the right of the people peaceably to assemble, and to petition the government for a redress of grievances.

AMENDMENT II [1791]   *(Right to Bear Arms)*

A well-regulated militia being necessary to the security of a free State, the right of the people to keep and bear arms shall not be infringed.

AMENDMENT III [1791]   *(Quartering of Soldiers)*

No soldier shall, in time of peace, be quartered in any house without the consent of the owner, nor in time of war, but in a manner to be prescribed by law.

AMENDMENT IV [1791]   *(Freedom of Persons)*

(Warrants, Searches, and Seizure)

The right of the people to be secure in their persons, houses, papers, and effects, against unreasonable searches and seizures, shall not be violated, and no warrants shall issue but upon probable cause, supported by oath or affirmation, and particularly describing the place to be searched, and the persons or things to be seized.

AMENDMENT V [1791]   *(Capital Crimes)*

(Protection of the Accused; Compensation)

No person shall be held to answer for a capital or otherwise infamous crime, unless on a presentment or indictment of a grand jury, except in cases arising in the land or naval forces, or in the militia, when in actual service in time of war or public danger; nor shall any person be subject for the same offense to be twice put in jeopardy of life or limb, nor shall be compelled in any criminal case to be a witness against himself, nor be deprived of life, liberty, or property, without due process of law; nor shall private property be taken for public use without just compensation.

AMENDMENT VI [1791]   *(Trial by Jury)*

(Accusation, Witnesses, Counsel)

In all criminal prosecutions, the accused shall enjoy the right to a speedy and public trial, by an impartial jury of the State and district wherein the crime shall have been committed, which district shall have been previously ascertained by law, and to be informed of the nature and cause of the accusation; to be confronted with the witnesses against him; to have compulsory process for obtaining witnesses in his favor, and to have the assistance of counsel for his defense.

AMENDMENT VII [1791]   *(Civil Law)*

In suits at common law, where the value in controversy shall exceed twenty dollars, the right of trial by jury shall be preserved, and no fact tried by a jury shall be otherwise reexamined in any court of the United States, than according to the rules of the common law.

AMENDMENT VIII [1791]   *(Bails, Fines, and Punishments)*

Excessive bail shall not be required, nor excessive fines imposed, nor cruel and unusual punishments inflicted.

AMENDMENT IX [1791] *(Rights Retained by the People)*

The enumeration in the Constitution, of certain rights, shall not be construed to deny or disparage others retained by the people.

AMENDMENT X [1791]   *(Rights Reserved to the States)*

The powers not delegated to the United States by the Constitution, nor prohibited by it to the States, are reserved to the States respectively, or to the people.

AMENDMENT XI [1798]   *(Jurisdictional Limits)*

The judicial power of the United States shall not be construed to extend to any suit in law or equity, commenced or prosecuted against one of the United States by citizens of another State, or by citizens or subjects of any foreign state.

AMENDMENT XII [1804]   *(Electoral College)*

The electors shall meet in their respective States, and vote by ballot for President and Vice President, one of whom, at least, shall not be an inhabitant of the same State with themselves; they shall name in their ballots the person voted for as President, and in distinct ballots the person voted for as Vice President, and they shall make distinct lists of all persons voted for as President, and of all persons voted for as Vice President, and of the number of votes for each, which lists they shall sign and certify, and transmit sealed to the seat of government of the United States, directed to the President of the Senate;—the President of the Senate shall, in the presence of the Senate and House of Representatives, open all the certificates and the votes shall then be counted;—the person having the greatest number of votes for President shall be the President, if such number be a majority of the whole number of electors appointed; and if no person have such majority, then from the persons having the highest numbers not exceeding three on the list of those voted for as President, the House of Representatives shall choose immediately, by ballot, the President. But in choosing the President, the votes shall be taken by States, the representation from each State having one vote; a quorum for this purpose shall consist of a member or members from two-thirds of the States, and a majority of all the States shall be necessary to a choice. And if the House of Representatives shall not choose a President whenever the right of choice shall devolve upon them, before *the fourth day of March* next following, then the Vice President shall act as President, as in the case of the death or other constitutional disability of the

The Constitution of the United States, continued

President.

The person having the greatest number of votes as Vice President shall be the Vice President, if such number be a majority of the whole number of electors appointed; and if no person have a majority, then from the two highest numbers on the list the Senate shall choose the Vice President; a quorum for the purpose shall consist of two-thirds of the whole number of Senators, and a majority of the whole number shall be necessary to a choice. But no person constitutionally ineligible to the office of President shall be eligible to that of Vice President of the United States.

AMENDMENT XIII [1865] *(Abolition of Slavery)*

Section 1. Neither slavery nor involuntary servitude, except as a punishment for crime whereof the party shall have been duly convicted, shall exist within the United States, or any place subject to their jurisdiction.

Section 2. Congress shall have power to enforce this article by appropriate legislation.

AMENDMENT XIV [1868] *(Citizenship)*

(Due Process of Law)
Section 1. All persons born or naturalized in the United States, and subject to the jurisdiction thereof, are citizens of the United States and of the State wherein they reside. No State shall make or enforce any law which shall abridge the privileges or immunities of citizens of the United States; nor shall any State deprive any person of life, liberty, or property, without due process of law; nor deny to any person within its jurisdiction the equal protection of the laws.

(Apportionment; Right to Vote)
Section 2. Representatives shall be apportioned among the several States according to their respective numbers, counting the whole number of persons in each State, excluding Indians not taxed. But when the right to vote at any election for the choice of Electors for President and Vice President of the United States, Representatives in Congress, the executive and judicial officers of a State, or the members of the legislature thereof, is denied to any of the male inhabitants of such State, being twenty-one years of age and citizens of the United States, or in any way abridged, except for participation in rebellion, or other crime, the basis of representation therein shall be reduced in the proportion which the number of such male citizens shall bear to the whole number of male citizens twenty-one years of age in such State.

(Disqualification for Office)
Section 3. No person shall be a Senator or Representative in Congress, or Elector of President and Vice President, or hold any office, civil or military, under the United States, or under any State, who, having previously taken an oath, as a member of Congress, or as an officer of the United States, or as a member of any State legislature, or as an executive or judicial officer of any State, to support the Constitution of the United States, shall have engaged in insurrection or rebellion against the same, or given aid or comfort to the enemies thereof. Congress may, by a vote of two-thirds of each house, remove such disability.

(Public Debt)
Section 4. The validity of the public debt of the United States, authorized by law, including debts incurred for payment of pensions and bounties for services in suppressing insurrection or rebellion, shall not be questioned. But neither the United States nor any State shall assume or pay any debt or obligation incurred in aid of insurrection or rebellion against the United States, or any claim for the loss of emancipation of any slave; but all such debts, obligations, and claims shall be held illegal

and void.

Section 5. The Congress shall have power to enforce, by appropriate legislation, the provisions of this article.

AMENDMENT XV [1870]   *(Right to Vote)*

Section 1. The right of citizens of the United States to vote shall not be denied or abridged by the United States or by any State on account of race, color, or previous condition of servitude.

Section 2. The Congress shall have power to enforce this article by appropriate legislation.

AMENDMENT XVI [1913]   *(Income Tax)*

The Congress shall have power to lay and collect taxes on incomes, from whatever source derived, without apportionment among the several States, and without regard to any census or enumeration.

AMENDMENT XVII [1913]   *(Senators)*

(Election)

Section 1. The Senate of the United States shall be composed of two Senators from each State, elected by the people thereof, for six years; and each Senator shall have one vote. The electors in each State shall have the qualifications requisite for electors of [voters for] the most numerous branch of the State legislatures.

(Vacancies)

Section 2. When vacancies happen in the representation of any State in the Senate, the executive authority of such State shall issue writs of election to fill such vacancies: Provided that the legislature of any State may empower the executive thereof to make temporary appointments until the people fill the vacancies by election as the legislature

may direct.

Section 3. This amendment shall not be so construed as to affect the election or term of any Senator chosen before it becomes valid as part of the Constitution.

AMENDMENT XVIII [1919]   *(Prohibition)*

Section 1. After one year from the ratification of this article the manufacture, sale, or transportation of intoxicating liquors within, the importation thereof into, or the exportation thereof from the United States and all territory subject to the jurisdiction thereof, for beverage purposes, is hereby prohibited.

Section 2. The Congress and the several States shall have concurrent power to enforce this article by appropriate legislation.

Section 3. This article shall be inoperative unless it shall have been ratified as an amendment to the Constitution by the legislatures of the several States, as provided by the Constitution, within seven years from the date of the submission thereof to the States by the Congress.

AMENDMENT XIX [1920]   *(Women's Suffrage)*

Section 1. The right of citizens of the United States to vote shall not be denied or abridged by the United States or by any State on account of sex.

Section 2. The Congress shall have power to enforce this article by appropriate legislation.

AMENDMENT XX [1933]   *(Terms of Office)*

Section 1. The terms of the President and Vice President shall end at noon on the 20th day of January, and the terms of Senators and Representatives at noon on the 3d day of January, of the years in which such terms would have ended if this article

The Constitution of the United States, continued

had not been ratified; and the terms of their successors shall then begin.

Section 2. The Congress shall assemble at least once in every year, and such meeting shall begin at noon on the 3d day of January, unless they shall by law appoint a different day.

(Succession)

Section 3. If, at the time fixed for the beginning of the term of the President, the President-elect shall have died, the Vice President-elect shall become President. If a President shall not have been chosen before the time fixed for the beginning of his term, or if the President-elect shall have failed to qualify, then the President-elect shall act as President until a President shall have qualified; and the Congress may by law provide for the case wherein neither a President-elect nor a Vice President-elect shall have qualified, declaring who shall then act as President, or the manner in which one who is to act shall be selected, and such persons shall act accordingly until a President or Vice President shall have qualified.

Section 4. The Congress may by law provide for the case of the death of any of the persons from whom the House of Representatives may choose a President whenever the right of choice shall have devolved upon them, and for the case of the death of any of the persons from whom the Senate may choose a Vice President whenever the right of choice shall have devolved upon them.

Section 5. Sections 1 and 2 shall take effect on the 15th day of October following the ratification of this article.

Section 6. This article shall be inoperative unless it shall have been ratified as an amendment to the Constitution by the legislatures of three-fourths of the several States within seven years from the date of its submission.

AMENDMENT XXI [1933] *(Prohibition Repealed)*

Section 1. The eighteenth article of amendment to the Constitution of the United States is hereby repealed.

Section 2. The transportation or importation into any State, Territory, or Possession of the United States for delivery or use therein of intoxicating liquors, in violation of the laws thereof, is hereby prohibited.

Section 3. This article shall be inoperative unless it shall have been ratified as an amendment to the Constitution by conventions in the several States, as provided in the Constitution, within seven years from the date of submission thereof to the States by the Congress.

AMENDMENT XXII [1951] *(Term of President)*

Section 1. No person shall be elected to the office of President more than twice, and no person who has held the office of President, or acted as President, for more than two years of a term to which some other person is elected President shall be elected to the office of President more than once. But this article shall not apply to any person holding the office of President when this article was proposed by the Congress, and shall not prevent any person who may be holding the office of President, or acting as President, during the term within which this article becomes operative from holding the office of President or acting as President during the remainder of such term.

Section 2. This article shall be inoperative unless it shall have been ratified as an amendment to the Constitution by the legislatures of three-fourths of the several States within seven years from the date of its submission to the States by the Congress.

AMENDMENT XXIII [1961]
(Washington, D.C.)

(Enfranchisement of Voters in Federal Elections)

Section 1. The District constituting the seat of Government of the United States shall appoint in such manner as the Congress may direct:

A number of electors of President and Vice President equal to the whole number of Senators and Representatives in Congress to which the District would be entitled if it were a State, but in no event more than the least populous State; they shall be in addition to those appointed by the States, but they shall be considered for the purposes of the election of President and Vice President, to be electors appointed by a State; and they shall meet in the District and perform such duties as provided by the twelfth article of amendment.

Section 2. The Congress shall have the power to enforce this article by appropriate legislation.

AMENDMENT XXIV [1964]   (Poll Tax)

Section 1. The right of citizens of the United States to vote in any primary or other election for President or Vice President, for electors for President or Vice President, or for Senator or Representative in Congress, shall not be denied or abridged by the United States or any State by reason of failure to pay any poll tax or other tax.

Section 2. The Congress shall have the power to enforce this article by appropriate legislation.

AMENDMENT XXV [1967]
(Succession)

Section 1. In case of the removal of the President from office or of his death or resignation, the Vice President shall become President.

Section 2. Whenever there is a vacancy in the office of the Vice President, the President shall nominate a Vice President who shall take office upon confirmation by a majority vote of both houses of Congress.

Section 3. Whenever the President transmits to the President pro tempore of the Senate and the Speaker of the House of Representatives his written declaration that he is unable to discharge the power and duties of his office, and until he transmits to them a written declaration to the contrary, such powers and duties shall be discharged by the Vice President as Acting President.

Section 4. Whenever the Vice President and a majority of either the principal officers of the executive departments or of such other body as Congress may by law provide, transmit to the President pro tempore of the Senate and the Speaker of the House of Representatives their written declaration that the President is unable to discharge the powers and duties of his office, the Vice President shall immediately assume the powers and duties of the office as Acting President.

Thereafter, when the President transmits to the President pro tempore of the Senate and the Speaker of the House of Representatives his written declaration that no inability exists, he shall resume the powers and duties of his office unless the Vice President and a majority of either the principal officers of the executive departments or of such other body as Congress may by law provide, transmit within four days to the President pro tempore of the Senate and the Speaker of the House of Representatives their written declaration that the President is unable to discharge the powers and duties of his office. Thereupon Congress shall decide the issue, assembling within forty-eight hours for that purpose if not in session. If the Congress, within twenty-one days after receipt of the latter written declaration, or, if Congress is not in session, within twenty-one days after Congress is required to assemble, determines by two-thirds vote of both Houses that the President is unable to discharge the powers and duties of his office, the Vice President shall continue to discharge the same as Acting President; otherwise, the President shall resume the powers and duties of his office.

AMENDMENT XXVI [1971] *(18-Year-Old Vote)*

Section 1. The right of citizens of the United States, who are eighteen years of age or older, to vote shall not be denied or abridged by the United States or by any State on account of age.

Section 2. The Congress shall have power to enforce this article by appropriate legislation.

AMENDMENT XXVII [1992] *(Congressional Pay Raises)*

No law, varying the compensation for the services of the Senators and Representatives, shall take effect, until an election of Representatives shall have intervened.

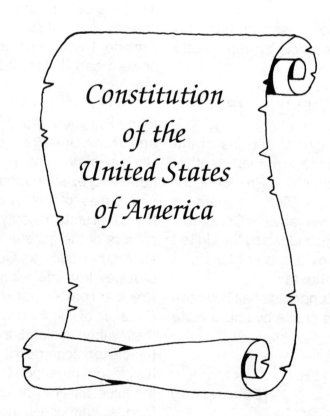

Constitution of the United States of America